1 MONTH OF FREE READING

at

www.ForgottenBooks.com

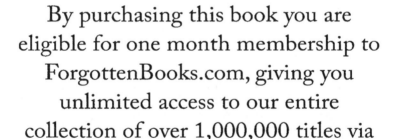

By purchasing this book you are eligible for one month membership to ForgottenBooks.com, giving you unlimited access to our entire collection of over 1,000,000 titles via our web site and mobile apps.

To claim your free month visit:

www.forgottenbooks.com/free766460

ISBN 978-0-656-32875-8
PIBN 10766460

This book is a reproduction of an important historical work. Forgotten Books uses
state-of-the-art technology to digitally reconstruct the work, preserving the original format
whilst repairing imperfections present in the aged copy. In rare cases, an imperfection in
the original, such as a blemish or missing page, may be replicated in our edition. We do,
however, repair the vast majority of imperfections successfully; any imperfections that
remain are intentionally left to preserve the state of such historical works.

Historic, archived document

Do not assume content reflects current
scientific knowledge, policies, or practices.

Dreer's Mid=summer Catalogue

1897

Pot=Grown

Strawberry Plant

Celery and other Seasonable

Plants, Seeds, etc

HENRY A. DREER, 714 Chestnut Street, Philadelphia, P.

M. D. WOOD PRINTING CO., PHILA.

DREER'S MID=SUMMER CATALOGUE

June—1897—August

We take-pleasure in presenting our Mid-Summer List for the current year, offering a choice selection of the very best varieties of pot-grown Strawberry plants for July to September planting. Also Celery, Cabbage and other plants, which are grown in large quantities at our Riverton Nurseries. All are strong, healthy, well-grown plants that are certain to give the best results. Included is a list of Vegetable and Flower seeds for Summer sowing.

AN INVITATION

We cordially invite our patrons to pay a visit to our extensive plant establishment at Riverton during the Summer. Many additional improvements have been made in the past year. The new ponds of Water Lilies will be an attraction to lovers of this beautiful class of plants, and the great display of summer blooming plants including the latest varieties of Crozy's French Cannas, New Cactus and Double Dahlias, and our famous strain of double fringed Petunias, etc. Time Tables on application.

GENERAL DIRECTIONS TO CORRESPONDENTS.

REMITTANCES should be made by Post Office Money Order, Drafts on Philadelphia or New York Banks, or Express Money Orders. We disclaim all responsibility when remittances are not made as above directed. Where it is not possible to obtain these, the letters should be registered. Postage stamps will be found a convenient method of remitting for small amounts, and can be used by us to advantage. Coin should not be sent by mail.

CASH WITH ORDER.—Please send money with the order sufficient to cover the whole bill to facilitate the execution of your orders. During the busy season, to make out bills for customers, charge, and in a few days receive the money, make the proper credit and send receipt, requires more work than we can readily perform.

NEW CUSTOMERS.—Orders from parties unknown to us must be accompanied by a remittance or by satisfactory reference to some responsible house, or to some person of our acquaintance. We decline sending goods "Collect on Delivery" to parties unknown to us unless remittance be made on account to guarantee acceptance.

POSTAGE PAID.—We deliver, postage paid, to any Post Office in the United States, **Vegetable and Flower Seeds, in Packets, Ounces and Pounds**, also Bulbs and Plants, when ordered at Catalogue prices, except where otherwise noted. *No orders for plants by mail will be accepted for less than 50 cents in value.*

LOW EXPRESS RATES ON PLANTS.—We are shipping by all express lines to any part of the country, plants packed in closed boxes at a reduction of 20 per cent. from regular rates of merchandise. Boxes weighing less than 100 pounds are charged at pound rates, minimum charge not less than 35 cents. For example : where the general rate is $5.00 per 100 pounds, a box weighing 20 pounds will be carried for 80 cents. Prepaid 4 pound packages of seeds, plants and bulbs are carried to California and all distant points for 30 cents each.

BAGGAGE=MASTER DELIVERIES are very convenient to points within twenty-five miles of Philadelphia. Charges for packages not exceeding 10 lbs. 5 cents, 25 lbs. 10 cents, 50 lbs. 15 cents.

PACKING.—No charge is made for boxes or packing, nor for delivery to Freight Depots or Express Office.

NON=WARRANTY.—We wish it to be distinctly understood that although we continue to take all possible pains to supply only New, Genuine and Unadulterated Seeds and Plants, we still give no warranty, express or implied, as to description, quality, productiveness or any other matter of any of the Seeds or Plants we send out, and will not be in any way responsible for the crop. Every order received for articles named in this Catalogue will be executed on these conditions only.

HENRY A. DREER, 714 Chestnut Street,

GREENHOUSES AND NURSERIES, RIVERTON, N. J.   PHILADELPHIA, PA.

POT=GROWN ➤ Strawberry Plants

Planted too Deep

Wrong Way of Planting

Pot=Grown plants set out this summer will produce a FULL CROP of fruit next June.

Our facilities for growing Strawberry Plants at our Nursery and Trial Farm at Riverton enable us to test all recently introduced and promising new varieties with the view of offering only such as show decided merit.

➤ TIME OF SHIPMENT ➤

Our pot-grown Strawberry plants are ready for shipment the latter part of July, and can be supplied as late as October in such varieties as are unsold at that time.

It is better, however, to procure the plants in August or September, as earlier plantings will develop larger and more vigorous plants and produce a greater crop of fruit next year.

Directions for Garden Culture

Too Shallow Planting.

To cultivate strawberries for family use, we recommend a thorough preparation of the ground by spading or plowing. Work into the soil a liberal quantity of well-rotted manure. Use also, our brands of ground bone and wood ashes. Plant in rows two feet apart; the plants fifteen inches apart in rows. Pinch off all runners. Cultivate frequently. In December, cover the entire bed an inch deep with straw or long litter from the stable. In late March, remove litter from crowns of the plants, but not from the alleys. Use sufficient straw about plants to keep the berries clean. This is the "hill" system of strawberry growing, and is especially adapted to summer and autumn planting. It involves the most work, but produces finest berries and largest crop from a given area.

Right Way of Planting.

The "matted row" plan, more especially suited to spring planting, is used by all market gardeners, and is adapted to family gardens also. It is substantially as follows:—Prepare the ground as above. Set the plants in rows three feet apart, and fifteen inches apart in rows; permit runners to form and take root; cultivate the alleys continually, as close to the plants as possible, finally making alley and row each about eighteen inches in width. Keep the bed wholly free of weeds. Cover in winter, as above, and in March, uncover crowns of plants. Use plenty of mulching, so as to keep berries clean, and ground moist and cool.

PERFECT AND IMPERFECT OR PISTILLATE FLOWERS

Pistillate or Imperfect Blossom.

Varieties marked pistillate have imperfect blossoms. They include many of the most prolific and desirable kinds. It is only necessary to plant perfect-flowered varieties near them, in the proportion of one to four; either one plant to four in the row, or one row of staminate or perfect flowering plants to four rows of pistillate plants. Hints on varieties adapted to purposes of fertilization will be found in each case where fertilization is needed.

Bi-sexual or Perfect Blossom.

Pot=Grown ➤ "versus" ➤ Layer Plants

Potted plants may appear expensive, yet when the labor necessary to grow them into proper condition and the time saved in the result of the crop are considered, they will be found much cheaper than ordinary layer plants. They may be planted after a crop of early summer vegetables has been harvested, and a crop of fruit secured in eight or ten months after planting.

We forward by express at the purchaser's expense. The plants are packed compactly, and as light as possible, and we recommend purchasers to have their orders forwarded in this manner.

No charge for boxes or packing.

Pot-Grown Strawberry Plant.

Layer Plants.

A full list of layer plants will be announced in September. They are not so desirable as pot-grown plants and will not produce as large a crop of fruit next spring; but they are cheaper, and more available for extensive plantings. Under proper autumn treatment they will produce quite satisfactory results.

NOTE.—A "layer" strawberry plant is one that has taken root by its own effort, whereas a "pot-grown" plant has been aided by human skill in making strong and compact roots. The "pot-grown" plant is stronger to begin with, and its growth is not checked by transplanting it.

A Quartette of
New Strawberries

All pot-grown plants, which if planted this summer will produce a full crop of berries next June.

Of the legion of new strawberries which we tested in our experimental grounds at Riverton, N. J. the past season, the four varieties offered below combined in a superlative degree, those qualities which go to make up the "ideal" strawberry, all being strong, vigorous growers, heavy croppers, with large and handsome fruits, of fine color and most delicious flavor, and for private gardens where "fancy" fruit is appreciated we feel sure they will become favorites.

I X L. Late, Pistillate.

A seedling raised at Pensauken, N. J., having many valuable characteristics, the plant is a good strong grower, with dark green foliage and nearly rust-proof, extraordinarily productive even in light soil, the fruit is borne on long stems standing up well from the ground and are of large size and of a most brilliant scarlet color. The flavor is slightly tart but very good, a grand berry for the private garden, its fine color and general excellence making it a fine desert fruit. Fertilize with Saunders, Sharpless or other perfect flowering sort. Pot-grown plants, 75 cents per dozen, $6.00 per hundred.

Crescent Improved. Mid-Season, Pistillate.

This variety is a decided improvement on the well-known Crescent seedling, which has been well named the "Lazy Man's Berry" because no amount of neglect would prevent it from bearing a crop, although, with good treatment it has been as satisfactory as any. The "Improved" is superior in every way to the type, the fruit being uniformly large, all ripening up, and of exquisite flavor, it should be planted in conjunction with Woolverton, Saunders or other perfect flowered sort to thoroughly pollenize it. Worthy of a trial, whether intended for home or market. Pot-grown plants, 75 cents per dozen, $6.00 per hundred.

Glen Mary. Mid-Season to Late, Imperfectly Bi-sexual.

Originated in Eastern Pennsylvania, and is described by a large grower as follows: "'I have known it since its first bearing, and firmly believe it deserves the title of 'the berry-grower's moneymaker.' It makes a very strong plant, but few of them. This reduces the cost of keeping the row in proper shape for fruiting. Its roots are enormous, enabling it to ripen its great crop of monster berries in the driest season. It has never been injured by the winter even without mulch, and has never failed to produce a large crop of fruit. The flower is imperfectly bi-sexual, but has always been grown alone by the originator; though I think the berries are rather more perfect when grown with the Brandywine, the two varieties blooming together through a long season.

The berries ripen from mid-season to late; are firm enough to ship well; of good quality, though not so pronounced as the Brandywine, but many prefer them to the latter. In size they are more uniformly large than any other variety." Should be in every garden. Pot-grown plants 75 cents per dozen, $6.00 per hundred.

Gandy Belle. Mid-Season, Perfect.

For the family supply or markets that like dark, glossy red berries this variety stands at the head of the list. The plant is a good grower, perfectly healthy, has a perfect blossom, and is a good bearer. The fruit is large and very handsome, somewhat acid, but of rich, high flavor, ripening early and extending well into mid-summer. An extra choice strawberry. Pot-grown plants 75 cents per dozen, $6.00 per hundred.

COLLECTIONS OF NEW STRAWBERRIES.

3	Each of the above four varieties (pot-grown) for	$ .75
6	" " " " " " "	1.25
12	" " " " " " "	2.50

THE FOUR SEASONS STRAWBERRY 🌿 🌿

Fraise des Quatre Saisons

A native of the European Alps, and distinguished by the property (which is peculiar to it) of producing flowers and fruits continuously all through the summer. The introduction of this variety into European gardens is comparatively recent, but it speedily attained a very important position, on account of its valuable quality of producing fruit at a season when all other varieties of strawberries have long ceased bearing, it being possible to secure good crops of berries during July, August and September. The fruit, while not large, are of exquisite flavor. No doubt many of our customers have enjoyed these delicious berries when in Europe. We advise planting them in a partially shaded position, and in order to secure a prolonged and abundant supply in late summer and autumn the flowering stems and runners should be pinched off through the spring months and the plants kept growing by an abundant supply of water. There are two varieties, red and white fruiting ; we can supply strong, pot-grown plants of either. Price 50 cents per dozen, $4.00 per hundred.

FOUR SEASONS STRAWBERRY.

Dreer's 🌿 🌿 Collection of Six Superb Pot-Grown Plants ⟶ Strawberries

While we do not offer a long list of varieties, our stock includes the very best so far as careful selection and test can secure the highest quality. Scores of new strawberries come upon the market every year, of which but few have permanent merit. Each season we add to our list all the better sorts which come forward with well-endorsed claims to public favor, and each season drop from our catalogue those which have failed to fulfil the claims made by their friends.

Notwithstanding the care we take in keeping our list down so as to include only varieties of sterling merit, the amateur finds difficulty in making a selection that will produce a bountiful supply of the finest fruit from the beginning to the end of the season. It is for such that we offer this collection, which, in our judgment, based on actual tests made on our experimental grounds, combine in the highest degree all the qualities which high-grade strawberries should have.

Superb Early Sorts.	Superb Mid-Season Sorts.	Superb Late Sorts.
MARSHALL, described on page 6	ENHANCE, described on page 4	BRANDYWINE, described on p. 4
HAVERLAND, " " 5	GREENVILLE, " " 5	TIMBRELL, " " 7

3 each of the Six Superb Strawberries, 18 pot-grown plants for	. . . .	$ .75
6 " " " " 36 " "	. . . .	1.50
12 " " " " 72 " "	. . . .	2.50
25 " " " " 150 " "	. . . .	4.50
50 " " " " 300 " "	. . . .	8.00

COLLECTION OF SELECT TESTED STRAWBERRIES.

☞ Pot=Grown Plants. ☜

This collection is offered for such as wish to try for themselves the merits of all the varieties which we offer on pages 4 to 7 :

3 each of the 23 varieties 69 pot-grown plants for	. . . .	$ 2.50
6 " " 23 " 138 " "	. . . .	4.50
12 " " 23 " 276 " "	. . . .	8.50
25 " " 23 " 575 " "	. . . .	15.00

General List of Select Tested
Pot=Grown Strawberry Plants

If planted before the middle of September these will produce a full crop next June.

While we do not offer a long list of varieties, our stock includes the very best so far as careful selection and test can secure the highest quality. Scores of new strawberries come upon the market every year of which but few have permanent merit. Each season we add to our list all the better sorts which come forward with well endorsed claims to public favor, and each season drop from our catalogue those which have failed to fulfil the claims made by their friends.

Reduction in Prices. Please note the reduction in prices in the popular standard sorts. This is made possible by our production of these plants in great quantity, We have perfect facilities for packing and shipping pot-grown strawberry plants in summer and autumn. Remember that pot-grown plants, if set firmly in the ground, will safely endure anything except excessive or prolonged drought, and we advise immediate preparation and early planting (August) of next year's fruiting bed. Later planting is safe, but the stronger the growth this autumn, the larger will be the berry crop of 1898.

Bederwood. Early, Perfect.

A well-known early berry, a good strong grower and most prolific producer of regular conical shaped medium to large fruit, color orange scarlet and of excellent flavor. Never fails to produce fine crops. 50 cents per dozen; $3.00 per 100; $25.00 per 1000.

Brandywine. Late, Perfect.

All growers are unanimous in their praise of this magnificent berry, and it is now considered the finest of all late fruiting sorts. We do not know that it has a single defect, plants of extra strong constitution and growth doing well everywhere. The fruit is extra large, heart shaped, color bright, rich red, and the flavor leaves nothing to be desired. A grand variety for preserving, retaining its native flavor in a wonderful degree when canned. It always produces satisfactory crops, and whether grown for market or home consumption will always be found in the front rank of high grade berries. 50 cents per dozen; $3.00 per 100; $25.00 per 1000.

Bubach. Mid-Season, Pistillate.

One of the most productive berries now grown near Philadelphia, and one of the most profitable. The Bubach is in high favor among gardeners in both Pennsylvania and New Jersey, and is a recognized money maker. It has both size and quality. This berry occupied the post of honor on the Philadelphia stalls this year. It was the handsomest fruit on sale in the markets. Plant Sharpless or other perfect flowering variety to insure the fertility of the blossoms. Edgar Conrow, of Moorestown, N. J., votes Bubach the first place for profit. Michael Flynn, Moorestown, N. J.; Charles Bell, Mt. Ephraim, N. J.; James Q. Atkinson, Montgomery county, Pa., endorse this opinion. 50 cents per dozen; $3.00 per 100; $25.00 per 1000.

Charles Downing. Mid-Season, Perfect.

A grand old variety for the home garden, a good free grower, bearing good crops of medium-sized conical light red berries of the most exquisite flavor. Succeeds in all localities. Too soft for a market berry. 50 cents per dozen; $3.00 per 100; $25.00 per 1000.

Crawford. Mid-Season, Perfect.

Named after the well-known strawberry specialist, M. Crawford, who describes it as "a berry for amateurs who give good culture, for size, quality and beauty, it is one of the best, but it will not bear neglect. The plant is a good grower and bearer, has a perfect blossom and produces an abundance of very fine fruit. The berries are large, conical, dark red, glossy, firm, and very good." 60 cents per dozen; $4.00 per 100; $30.00 per 1000.

Enhance. Mid-Season, Perfect.

A grand berry either for home use canning, or for market, always bringing a fancy price. Plant vigorous, producing fine crops of largest size handsome berries of attractive bright crimson color, quality excellent, slightly acid but not sour. 50 cents per dozen; $3.00 per 100; $25.00 per 1000.

Gandy's Prize. Late, Perfect.

(See colored illustration on Front Cover).

A strong, healthy plant, needing rich soil for its perfect development. One of the best berries for late market. Fruit solid and fit for shipment to distant markets. Berry of fine flavor. The berries are borne upon long, strong stalks, well above the ground. "Best when fully ripe," says Mr. Rudolph Bingham, of Camden, N. J. Mr. Edwin Satterthwaite, the leading grower of Eastern Pennsylvania, has fifteen acres of Gandy strawberries on his farm at Jenkintown. It is his leading berry at this time. Under his high culture it is a money maker. Walter Yahn, market gardener, Olney, likes Gandy best. 50 cents per dozen; $3.00 per 100; $25.00 per 1000.

Gov. Hoard. Early to Mid-Season, Perfect.

Originated in Wisconsin, an excellent sort, ripening early and continuing in bearing for a longer period than most varieties. On this account it is a good sort to plant in small gardens where only a few plants of one kind is wanted. Abundant cropper, fruit large and of splendid quality. 50 cents per dozen; $3.00 per 100; $25.00 per 1000.

Greenville. Mid-Season, Pistillate.

A very fine sort considered by many an improvement on the Bubach. The picture of this fine berry is from a photograph of a box from the patch of Mr. Albert Atkinson, of Three Tuns, Montgomery county, Pa. The plants are thrifty, and this year s crop was very satisfactory. Greenville bore the honors for productiveness at the Pennsylvania Agricultural Experiment Station in 1895. Fertilize with May King, Sharpless or other rather early perfect-flowering variety. 50 cents per dozen; $3.00 per 100; $25.00 per 1000.

Haverland. Early, Pistillate.

A vigorous plant of the Crescent type. Must be fertilized with some perfect flowering sort, as May King or Sharpless. Fruit stalks long. Enormously productive. "First choice decidedly," says William G. Embree, a West Chester, Pa., grower. Berries medium to large, of pale scarlet color, of good flavor, and so extremely prolific and showy that the Haverland is a wide favorite for home use or market. Its merits as a cropper make it one of the most profitable sorts. 50 cents per dozen; $3.00 per 100; $25.00 per 1000.

PARKER EARLE.

Lady Thompson. Early, Perfect.

A North Carolina favorite of undoubted merit, with a great record for productiveness and profit, now planted extensively in the Northern States. Several Pennsylvania and New Jersey market gardeners fruited it last year, and praise its early ripening qualities. Strong foliage; fruit of good quality. 50 cents per dozen; $3.00 per 100; $25.00 per 1000.

Marshall. Early, Perfect.

This sort did well with us the past season, and has become a favorite with many growers. Mr. Crawford, the strawberry expert, says of it: "It may be described by saying that it is perfect in every way. It has produced 3,000 quarts on one-third of an acre. The plant is very large and luxuriant, blossoms perfect, fruit of the largest size, good shape, dark, glossy red, and of very excellent quality." 50 cents per dozen; $3.00 per 100; $25.00 per 1000.

Mary. Early, Pistillate.

A comparatively new berry, widely on trial on account of its record. Early, large, productive, with strong foliage. Worthy of trial everywhere. Fertilize with May King, Sharpless, or some other comparatively early perfect-flowered sort. 60 cents per dozen; $4.00 per 100; $30.00 per 1000.

May King. Early, Perfect.

An old and justly famous standard sort. It bears a fair crop of medium-sized, bright scarlet berries, and is a reliable kind to plant for fertilizing the earlier pistillate varieties. 50 cents per dozen; $3.00 per 100; $25.00 per 1000.

Michel's Early. Early, Perfect.

A very strong growing, extra early variety, moderately productive, with many friends. Quality good, attractive in color, and worthy of a place in all gardens. 50 cents per dozen; $3.00 per 100; $25.00 per 1000.

Parker Earle. Late, Perfect.

A most wonderful producer, having yielded at the rate of 15,000 quarts to the acre. It succeeds everywhere under proper treatment. Berries are long, conical, regular and uniform, glossy red in color, and of good quality. The variety is of Southern origin, and, although it bears dry weather well, its best and most prolific results are obtained under high culture, rich manuring and irrigation. The plant usually sets more fruit than it can possibly perfect except with a copious water supply. "First choice" of Mr. Albert Atkinson, of Three Tuns, Montgomery county, Pa., in our recent canvass. 50 cents per dozen; $3.00 per 100; $25.00 per 1000.

Rio. Early, Perfect.

A recent introduction that is very highly recommended. It is of a rich, glossy color, medium size and very prolific. Recommended by the practical experience of Mr. Edward T. Ingram, West Chester, Pa. 50 cents per dozen; $3.00 per 100; $25.00 per 1000.

Our advice.

PLACE CHIEF RELIANCE upon standard strawberries of known excellence, but DO NOT BE AFRAID to test new varieties on your grounds. There is no better pleasure in strawberry growing than in selecting the prizes from the ripe fruit of the test bed.

Saunders. Mid-Season to Late, Perfect.

Berries of largest size. One of the most productive of our Philadelphia market berries this year. Deep red, and of good quality. "Nothing so successful as Saunders," says Mr. B. F. Osler, of Pensauken, New Jersey. "Saunders decidedly ahead," says the foreman in charge of Mr. Wilmer Atkinson's patch at Three Tuns, Pa. A berry of great commercial value. 50 cents per dozen; $3.00 per 100; $25.00 per 1000.

Sharpless. Mid-Season, Perfect.

This berry is no longer the best that can be obtained, but it has so many friends that it remains a favorite, especially in private gardens. It is doubtful whether anything of better flavor is on the market, but it will not produce as many quarts as some others. Charles Boileau, of Fox Chase, still adheres to it as a market berry, but he is an exception. It succeeds everywhere, but particularly in private gardens, under "hill" culture. 50 cents per dozen; $3.00 per 100; $25.00 per 1000.

Tennessee. Early to Mid-Season, Perfect.

A new berry of great promise. A seedling of Crescent and Sharpless. Perfect flowers and vigorous plants. Very productive. Size medium to large. Bright scarlet berries of fine quality. Season early to medium, like its parents. Suited to both family and market. Thrives on light soil. 50 cts. per dozen; $3.00 per 100; $25.00 per 1000.

Timbrell. Late, Pistillate.

In the section of country tributary to the Philadelphia market the Timbrell is not a favorite for commercial purposes, but we commend it to private gardeners who can give the plant high culture and extra good treatment. It has in many places made a fine record for size and productiveness, but its greatest feature is the flavor of its fruit, which ranks with the best. Fertilize with Sharpless. 50 cents per dozen; $3.00 per 100; $25.00 per 1000.

Warfield. Mid-Season to Late, Pistillate.

A very fine berry in every way. Plant strong, free grower, and should not be planted too closely, wonderfully prolific bearer, one of the Agricultural Experiment Stations placing it at the head of 150 varieties for yield. Berries medium size, very firm, color rich glossy red and of fine flavor. Considered by many growers the most profitable market berry. 50 cts. per dozen; $3.00 per 100; $25.00 per 1000.

Woolverton. Early to Mid-Season, Perfect.

A promising berry of Canadian origin. It is a strong grower, with perfect flower, and crops over a long season. Matures part of its crop before it is done blossoming. A large strawberry of attractive appearance and good quality. Mr. Satterthwaite (June 8) said of it: "Early and very satisfactory; have been picking it for two weeks; enormous crop." 60 cents per dozen; $4.00 per 100; $30.00 per 1000.

We call special attention to our collections of "SIX SUPERB" STRAWBERRIES offered on p. 3

CELERY PLANTS.

WHITE PLUME.

Celery plants can be supplied from June 15th to August 25th. We grow the following varieties, which we offer at the uniform price of

40 cents per hundred.
$3.00 per thousand.

(If wanted by mail, add 15c. per 100 for Postage).

Celery requires a moist, rich soil, and will not thrive in poor soil and dry situations. After the plants have attained a height of five or six inches they should be set out in rows three feet apart and six inches in the row. When twelve to fifteen inches high, the soil should be loosened by the use of the plow or hoe and the plants be "handled." This operation consists of drawing the stems upright with one hand, and pressing the soil firmly against the plant with the other; by this process the plants grow upright, and can be easily cultivated and blanched by drawing the soil close up to the plant. Celery should receive thorough cultivation if good results are desired. To store for winter use, select well drained ground, dig trenches one foot wide and deep enough to cover the tops of the plants. Pack the stalks in this in an upright position, covering with boards to shed the water, and in severe weather protect with straw or leaves.

Selected Golden Heart.

The best of the half dwarf varieties, stalks large and full; the heart is golden yellow, turning to a light color when blanched. Very solid, rich flavor and good keeper.

White Plume.

We offer a choice strain of this valuable and popular variety. The White Plume is unsurpassed for fall and early winter use, requiring very little earthing up to blanch it.

Golden Self=Blanching.

An early, beautiful and in every way desirable sort, requiring but little labor to blanch. The heart is a rich golden yellow, with light yellowish green outer leaves. Of dwarf, compact habit, rich nutty flavor, and an excellent sort for table decoration.

Giant Pascal.

A superior keeping sort. The stalks are very large, thick, solid, crisp, and of a rich, nutty flavor, free from any trace of bitterness; it blanches very easily and quickly, and retains its freshness a long time after being marketed. The heart is golden yellow, very full and attractive in appearance.

Perfection Heartwell.

A large, solid growing variety of excellent flavor and creamy white color. In size it is between the Golden Dwarf and White Solid. It is an excellent market sort, as the stalks are clear and attractive in color.

Boston Market.

An excellent half dwarf sort of vigorous and bushy habit, producing many side shoots. Blanches perfectly white, is very sweet, crisp and of excellent flavor.

Dwarf Rose.

The red sorts surpass the white in flavor, and possess in their coloring a feature which renders them valuable as a table ornament.

Price.

ANY OF THE ABOVE VARIETIES 40 CENTS PER 100; $3.00 PER 1000.

If wanted by mail add 15 cents per 100 for postage.

Miscellaneous Vegetable Plants.

IN STOCK FROM MIDDLE OF JUNE TILL AUGUST.

(Any of the following can be sent by mail at an additional cost of 15 cents per 100.)

DREER'S SELECTED LATE FLAT DUTCH.

CABBAGE

Dreer's Selected Late Flat Dutch.

Short stem and large, solid flat heads. Our stock has been carefully selected for several years in order to get a cabbage of this type, and we are confident no better strain is on the market. 40 cents per 100; $2.50 per 1000.

Lupton.

A new winter variety of excellent quality and distinct character; a little earlier than the above, but will maintain shape and solidity for storing; of compact growth, color dark green and very uniform head. 50 cents per 100; $3.50 per 1000.

RED CABBAGE.

Mammoth Rock Red.

The largest and most solid of the red varieties, a sure heading sort and tender. 40 cents per 100; $2.50 per 1000.

SAVOY CABBAGE.

Perfection Drumhead.

Of superior quality; the largest solid-heading Savoy, possessing the rich flavor of the Cauliflower. 40 cents per 100; $2.50 per 1000.

DREER'S SELECTED DWARF ERFURT CAULIFLOWER.

PERFECTION DRUMHEAD SAVOY CABBAGE.

CAULIFLOWER.

Dreer's Selected Dwarf Erfurt.

One of the earliest in cultivation; small-leaved dwarf, for forcing or open ground, producing very solid pure white heads of the finest quality. It grows about 15 inches high, and in ordinary seasons every plant will produce a marketable head. 75 cents per 100; $7.00 per 1000.

Early Snowball.

An extremely early dwarf variety, producing magnificent white heads of fine quality. Well adapted to hot-bed culture. 75 cents per 100; $7.00 per 1000.

BRUSSELS SPROUTS.

Dreer's Select Matchless.

A small-leaved variety of this notable vegetable, which, through careful selection has been brought to perfection; grows freely during the summer, and is fully developed by the early frosts, at which time the stems are thickly set with sprouts the full length. 50 cents per 100; $4.00 per 1,000.

DREER'S MATCHLESS BRUSSELS SPROUTS.

VEGETABLE SEEDS.

FOR SUMMER...,
AND FALL SOWING

The following list of vegetable seeds comprises the leading varieties suitable for present sowing. By sowing at intervals during the summer months a constant supply of fresh vegetables may be obtained until late in the fall. When beans and peas are to be sent by mail, add 15 cents and on sweet corn 10 cents per quart additional to price for postage. We pay postage on small seeds by the packet, ounce or quarter pound.

IMPROVED EARLY VALENTINE.

BEANS. Plant for succession up to the middle of August. **Dwarf or Bush.**

	Pt.	Qt.	Pk.
Improved, Early Valentine	.15	25	$1 25
Early Mohawk	.15	25	1 25
Long Yellow Six Weeks	.15	25	1 25
Extra Early Refugee	.15	25	1 00
White Kidney, or Royal Dwarf	.15	20	1 00
White Marrowfat	.15	20	1 00
Wonder of France	.15	30	1 50

Wax Varieties.

	Pt.	Qt.	Pk.
Imp. Prolific Black Wax	.15	25	1 25
Golden Wax Improved	.15	30	1 25
Wardwell's Kidney Wax	.15	30	1 25
Currie's Rust-proof	.15	30	1 75
Valentine Wax	.15	30	1 75
Early Refugee Wax	.15	30	1 75
Perfection Wax (Crimson Flageolet)	.15	30	1 50

BEETS, TABLE SORTS. Sow for succession up to August 1st.

	Pkt.	Oz.	¼ Lb.	Lb.
Early Eclipse	5	10	20	50
Early Egyptian Blood Turnip	5	10	20	50
Bastian's Extra Early Turnip	5	10	20	50
Lentz Extra Early Turnip	5	10	20	50
Edmand's Early Blood Turnip	5	10	20	50
Early Blood Turnip Improved	5	10	20	50
Bastian's Half Long Blood	5	10	20	50
Arlington Favorite	10	20	40	1 00

CARROT. Sow for main crop in June and July.

Early Scarlet Horn	5	10	20	75
Half Long Nantes	5	10	20	75
Early Half Long Scarlet, pointed	5	10	20	75
Danver's Half Long	5	10	20	75
Guerande, or Oxheart	5	10	20	75
Long Orange	5	10	20	75
Nichol's Long Orange	5	10	20	75

CAULIFLOWER. Sow for Autumn cutting up to July 15th.

	Pkt.	Oz.
Dreer's Earliest Snowstorm	.25	$5 00
Dreer's Selected Dwarf Erfurt	.20	2 50
Early Snowball	.20	2 50
Early Dwarf Erfurt	.10	1 50
Algiers	.10	75
Lenormand's Short Stemmed	.10	75

CORN SALAD.

	Pkt.	Oz.	¼ Lb.	Lb.
Large Leaved	5	10	20	50

CORN, SWEET. For succession plant every two weeks until the middle of July.

	Pt.	Qt.	Pk.
Extra Early White Cob Cory	15	25	$1 00
Crosby's Extra Early	15	20	80
Stabler's Extra Early	15	20	80
Stowell's Evergreen	15	20	80
Stabler's Nonpareil	15	20	80
Roslyn Hybrid	15	20	80
Mammoth	15	20	80

CUCUMBER. For pickles plant up to middle of July.

	Pkt.	Oz.	¼ Lb.	Lb.
Imp. Early White Spine	5	10	25	8 60
Arlington White Spine	5	10	30	1 00
Cool and Crisp	5	10	30	1 00
Early Cluster	5	10	25	60
Early Frame or Short Green	5	10	25	60
Early Russian	5	10	25	60
Green Prolific	5	10	25	60
Chicago Pickling	5	10	25	60
Small Gherkin or Burr	5	15	35	

ENDIVE. Sow for late use in July.

Giant Fringed	5	20	60	$2 00
Improved Green Curled	5	20	50	1 50
White Curled, Self-blanching	5	20	50	1 50
Broad-leaved Batavian (Escarolle)	5	20	50	1 50

KALE, or BORECOLE.

Dreer's Imperial	5	10	25	75
Dwarf Curled German	5	10	25	75
Dwarf Curled Scotch	5	10	25	75

KOHL RABI. Sow until August 1st. for Fall crop.

Earliest Erfurt	10	80	$1 00
Early White Vienna	5	25	60
Early Purple Vienna	5	20	60

DREER'S IMPROVED HANSON LETTUCE.

LETTUCE. For Summer sowing.

	Pkt.	Oz.	¼ Lb.	Lb.
Wonderful, a grand new large head variety	15			
Silver Ball	5	15	40	$1 50
Defiance, Summer	5	15	40	1 50
Dreer's Improved Hanson	5	15	40	1 50
Royal Summer Cabbage	5	15	40	1 50
Salamander	5	15	40	1 50
Yellow Seeded Butter	5	15	40	1 50
Deacon	5	15	40	1 50
California Cream Butter	5	15	40	1 50
Denver Market	5	15	40	1 50
Oak Leaved	5	15	40	1 50

PARSLEY.

	Pkt.	Oz.	¼ Lb.	Lb.
Half-curled	5	10	20	60
Dwarf Extra curled Perpetual	5	10	30	75
Champion Moss curled	5	10	30	75
Fern Leaved	5	10	30	90

PEAS. Good crops of Peas for Fall use may be secured by sowing the early sorts about the middle of August.

	Pt.	Qt.	Peck	Bush.
Dreer's Eureka Ex. Early	15	25	$1 25	$4 00
Improved Daniel O'Rourke	15	25	1 15	4 00
American Wonder	15	30	1 75	6 00
McLean's Little Gem	15	25	1 25	4 50
Premium Gem	15	25	1 25	4 50
McLean's Advancer	15	25	1 25	4 50
Dreer's Ex. Early Pioneer	15	25	1 25	4 00
Nott's Excelsior	15	30	2 00	
Lightning	15	25	1 25	4 00
Heroine	15	30	1 75	6 00
Champion of England	15	25	1 25	4 00
Admiral	15	30	1 50	5 50
Horsford's Market Garden	15	25	1 25	4 50

RADISH. Sow at intervals of two or three weeks until September for succession.

Early Varieties.

	Pkt.	Oz.	¼ Lb.	Lb.
Cardinal Globe	5	10	30	$1 00
White Tip, Scarlet Gem	5	10	25	75
Ex. Early White-tipped Scarlet Forcing	10	15	40	
Early Scarlet Turnip	5	10	20	60
Early French Breakfast	5	10	20	60
Half Long Scarlet	5	10	20	60
Philadelphia White Box	5	10	20	60
Cincinnati Market	5	10	30	1 00

RADISH--Continued.

Summer Varieties.

	Pkt.	Oz.	¼ Lb.	Lb.
Long White Vienna	5	10	25	75
White Delicacy	10	15	40	1 50
Beckert's Chartier	5	10	20	60
Long White Naples	5	10	20	60
White Summer Turnip	5	10	20	60
Golden Yellow, Olive-Shaped	5	10	30	1 00
Giant White Stuttgart	5	10	20	60
Yellow Summer Turnip	5	10	20	60
White Strasburg, extra	5	10	20	60

Winter Varieties.

Winter varieties should be sown in July and August.

Krewson's Oblong Black Spanish	5	10	30	$1 00
Long Black Spanish	5	10	20	60
Round Black Spanish	5	10	20	60
Large White Spanish	5	10	20	60
California White	5	10	25	75
Long Scarlet China	5	10	25	75
Round Scarlet China	10	20	60	2 00

SPINACH.

Victoria Long Standing	5	10	20	40
Long Standing, round seeded		5	10	30
Catillon Long Standing		5	10	30
Prickly Seeded		5	10	30
Dreer's Round Seeded Savoy		5	10	30
New Zealand		5	10	30	90

MUSHROOM SPAWN.

The best results are obtained by the use of our superior Mushroom Spawn, which is largely used by the most successful growers. Full and explicit instructions are contained in our circular, "How to Grow Mushrooms Successfully," which we will mail free on application.

Best English Milltrack Spawn. Per brick, 15 cents; 12 bricks, $1.75; 100 bricks, $12.50. By mail, 25 cents per brick.

French Spawn in 3 lb. boxes, $1.00. By mail, $1.25.

TURNIP==New Crop.

Sow in July and August for a Fall and Winter crop; do not sow later than the 1st of September; one ounce will sow 100 feet in drills; 2 pounds to the acre.

	Pkt.	Oz.	¼ Lb.	Lb.
White Flat Dutch		10	20	50
Red Top Strap-Leaf		10	20	50
Purple-Top White Globe		10	15	50
Ex. Early Purple-Top Milan		10	25	75
Early Snowball		10	25	75
Purple-Top Yellow Aberdeen		10	20	50
Large White Norfolk		10	15	40
Scarlet Kashmyr		15	50	1 50
Purple-Top Munich		10	20	60
White Egg		10	20	60
Golden Ball		10	20	60
Yellow or Amber Globe		10	20	60
Long White (Cow Horn)	5	10	20	50

RUTA BAGA TURNIP.

Dreer's Improved Purple-Top	5	10	25	75
American Purple Top	5	10	15	50
Skirving's Improved Purple-Top	5	10	20	50
Large White French	5	10	20	60
Budlong's Improved White	5	10	25	75

PURPLE-TOP WHITE GLOBE.

FARM SEEDS For Summer Sowing

Prices are subject to change without notice.

HUNGARIAN GRASS.

BUCKWHEAT.

Japanese, peck 40 cents, bus. (48 lbs.) . . $1.00
Silver Hull, peck 40 cents, bus. (48 lbs) . .90

MILLETS.

Golden or German Millet grows much taller than the Hungarian Grass, and produces larger crops. It also requires more time to grow, and a good soil. It makes a very coarse-looking, dry fodder, which is readily eaten by live stock. (50 pounds to the bushel). Per bus., $1.20. Five bus. and upwards at $1.10 per bus.

Hungarian Grass. An annual forage plant of great value. It flourishes during the heat of summer, remaining green when almost all other vegetation is dried up. It is one of the very best plants for green fodder, or for ensilaging, and makes hay of the best quality. Sow broadcast about one bushel of seed per acre, at any time from the middle of June till the first of August, (48 pounds to the bushel). Per bus., $1.20. Five bus. and upwards 1.10 per bus.

Egyptian or East India Pearl Millet. Lb. 20c.; 100 lbs. $15.00.

CLOVERS.

Crimson or Scarlet Clover. The crimson clover has become wonderfully popular both as a pasture and hay crop, also as a green manure for plowing in. It can be seeded at any time from June to October at the rate of 10 to 15 lbs. per acre and makes the earliest possible spring pasture, blooming the latter part of April or May, and for feeding as hay should be cut when in full bloom. If sown with Italian Rye Grass, which matures at the same time, it yields luxuriant and nutritious crops. Per pound, 8 cents (by mail 16 cents). Per bushel (60 lbs.) $3.50, 100 lbs. $5.50

Red or Medium	15c. per lb,	$10.00 per 100 lbs.
White Dutch Choice	25c.	"	20.00	"	"
Alfalfa, or Lucerne	15c.	"	12.00	"	"
Alsike	15c.	"	12.00	"	"

GRASSES.

Red Top Grass. Bus. (10 lb.) $1 ; bag, 50 lbs. $4.50 ; 100 lbs.	$ 8.00
Red Top Grass, Fancy (Free from chaff). Lb. 25c.; 100 lbs.	20.00
Kentucky Blue, Fancy. Bus. (14 lbs.) $2.25, per lb. 18c., per 100 lbs.	15.00
Wood Meadow Grass. Per lb. 40c., per 100 lbs.	30.00
Orchard Grass. Per bus. (14 lbs.) $2.50, per 100 lbs. . . .	16.00
Tall Meadow Oat Grass. Per lb. 20c., 100 lbs.	18.00
Crested Dogstail. Per lb.	.40
Sheep's Fescue. Per lb. 20c., per 100 lbs.	16.00
Meadow " " 12c., " "	10.00
Hard " " 20c., " "	16.00
Meadow Foxtail. " 40c., " "	35.00
Perennial Sweet Vernal. Per lb.	.50
Rough Stalked Meadow Grass. Per lb. 30c., per 100 lbs. . .	25.00
English Perennial Rye Grass. Per lb. 10c., per 100 lbs. $8.00, per bus. (24 lbs.)	2.25
Italian Rye Grass. Lb. 10c., 100 lbs. $8.00, bus. (22 lbs.) .	2.25
Rhode Island Bent. Per lb. 25c., per 100 lbs.	20.00
Canadian Blue. Per lb. 18c., per 100 lbs.	14.00
Timothy, Choice, Per bushel of 45 lbs.	2.50
" Prime " 45 "	2.25

MISCELLANEOUS FARM SEEDS.

	lb.	5 lbs.	10 lbs.
Mangel Wurzel, Mammoth Long-Red	.35	$1.50	$2.75
" Golden Tankard	.35	1.50	2.75
" Golden Mammoth	.35	1.50	2.75
" Norbiton Giant Red	.35	1.50	2.75
" Red Globe	.35	1.50	2.75
" Yellow or Orange Globe	.35	1.50	2.75
Sugar Cane or Sorghum, Early Amber. Per lb. 10c., per 100 lbs. . .			4.00
Johnson Grass (*Sorghum Halepense*). Per lb. 15c., per 100 lbs.			10.00
Rape. English Dwarf Essex. Per lb. 15c., per 10 lbs. $1.00, per 100 lbs.			8.00
Cow Peas. Southern Blackeye. Per peck 60c., per bus.			1.75
Canada Field Peas. Per peck 50c., per bus. $1.50, 10 bus. lots at . .			1.25
Sand or Winter Vetch. (*Vicia Sativa*) Per lb. 10c., per 100 lbs. . .			6.50
Flat Pea. (*Lathyrus Sylvestris*) Per lb.			2.00
Teosinte. (*Reana Luxurians*) Per oz. 15c., per lb.			1.25
Sunflower, large Russian. Per lb. 8c., per 100 lbs.			5.00
Lupine, Large Yellow. Per lb. 10c., per 100 lbs.			7.00

The above are all fully described in our Garden Calendar for 1897, a copy of which will be sent on application.

JAPANESE BUCKWHEAT

NATURAL SIZE.

Dreer's Reliable Flower Seeds.

The following list of Flower Seeds comprises a choice collection of Perennials that should be sown in the summer and fall for blooming next year. The Calceolaria, Cineraria, Primula, etc., for indoor blooming in the winter and spring, and the hardy varieties for blooming outdoors during the spring and summer months. Our selections of the seeds here offered are from world-renowned sources, and have always given the highest satisfaction.

CALCEOLARIA HYBRIDA GRANDIFLORA TIGRINA.

CARNATION, MARGUERITE.

ABUTILON.

Per pkt.

5010 Greenhouse shrubs of easy cultivation, beautiful drooping bell-shaped flowers; mixed colors 25

ACONITUM NAPELLUS.

5017. A hardy perennial, growing in any good garden soil, with very pretty blue and white flowers; 3 feet 5

ALYSSUM SAXATILE COMPACTUM.

5084 Showy golden-yellow flowers; hardy perennial; 1 foot 5

ANTIRRHINUM. Snap-Dragon.

The improved varieties of this valuable genus have large, finely-shaped flowers of the most brilliant colors.
5140 **Tom Thumb, Mixed,** finest dwarf. Per oz. 50c 5
5141 **Tall, Mixed,**   "   " 40c 5

AQUILEGIA. Columbine.

Beautiful hardy perennials, blooming freely early in the spring and summer; 1½ to 3 feet.
5143 **Chrysantha.** (*Golden-Spurred.*) Bright golden-yellow flowers 5
5144 **Cœrulea.** Violet-blue; inner petals pure white 10
5151 **Glandulosa.** Inner petals pure white; outer, a lovely shade of light blue 15
5160 **Single,** all colors mixed; per oz., 30 cents . . 5
5150 **Double,**   "   "   " 40 " . . 5

AURICULA.

5240 A well-known favorite of great beauty; seed saved from splendid choice varieties 15

CALCEOLARIA.

Gorgeous plants, producing a mass of beautiful pocket-like flowers early in the spring, a universal favorite for the greenhouse or conservatory. Sow end of July or in August.
5350 **Grandiflora, Mixed.** Large flowering, beautiful, rich, self-colored flowers; saved from a choice collection 25
5352 **Tigrina, Mixed.** Large-flowering, tigered and spotted flowers; the very finest mixture of the most brilliant colors 35

Per pkt.

5353 **Pumila Compacta.** Of dwarf, compact, robust growth, producing immense trusses of large and varied brilliant self-colored and spotted flowers 35

CAMPANULA. Bell-Flower.

5420 **Media, Single Mixed** (*Canterbury Bells*). Beautiful, large, bell-shaped flowers; 2½ feet . . . 5
5410 **Media, Double Mixed;** 2½ feet 5
5363 **Media Calycanthema** (*Cup and Saucer.*) . . . 10

HARDY PERENNIAL CANDYTUFT.

5388 **Iberis Sempervirens.** A profuse white blooming hardy perennial, adapted for rockeries, baskets, etc., coming in flower early in spring . . 10
5379 **Iberis Gibraltarica Hybrida.** Very fine species, with white flowers shading to lilac. 1 foot 10

CARNATION.

Carnations and Picotee Pinks are general favorites for their delicious fragrance and richness of color. The seeds we offer have been imported from the best sources in Europe, and will produce a large percentage of splendid double flowers.
5425 **Finest German.** Mixed colors; saved from extra fine double flowers 20
5426 **Remontant, or Tree.** (*Double Perpetual.*) Mixed colors; saved only from the finest and choicest double named varieties 25
5480 **Fine Double Mixed.** The hardiest and best varieties for open air culture 10
5423 **Early Flowering Double Vienna** 10
5428 **Marguerite.** Flowers in four months from seed and blooms continuously, great variety of colors and delightfully fragrant. Most desirable for cutting. ¼ oz., $1.00 10

CHRYSANTHEMUMS.

Very showy and popular flowers of easy culture. Seeds sown during the summer will produce blooming plants for autumn and winter decoration.
5488 **Frutescens Grandiflrum.** French Marguerites. Largely grown for cut flowers. They make elegant pot plants for winter flowering . 10
5480 **Inodorum Plenissimum.** Double snow-white, very free flowering and fine cutting 10

CINERARIA—DREER'S PRIZE DWARF.

CYCLAMEN PERSICUM GIGANTEUM.

CINERARIA.

Seed should be sown from May to September for succession. Where only one sowing is made July should be preferred.

	Per pkt.
5510 **Dreer's Prize Dwarf.** Mixed	35
5520 " " **Tall.** Mixed	35

The above strains of Cineraria cannot be surpassed either for size of flowers or beauty of color. Many of the blooms measure 2½ inches in diameter, and none will be smaller than a silver dollar.

5540 **Dwarf Choice.** Mixed	25
5530 **Tall** " " "	25
5550 **Double Mixed.** All the rich and beautiful colors of the single sorts exist in this selection . .	50

COREOPSIS LANCEOLATA.

5356 One of very best hardy perennials grown, with bright golden yellow flowers on long stems; excellent for cutting; flowering freely all summer   10

CYCLAMEN.

Charming plants with beautiful foliage and rich-colored fragrant flowers, universal favorites for winter and spring blooming.

5670 **Persicum, Choice Mixed.**	10
5660 " **Giganteum.** Mixed	25

DELPHINIUM.

One of our most showy and useful plants, possessing almost every requisite for the adornment of the garden; producing splendid spikes of flowers in profusion throughout the summer; hardy perennials.

5705 **Formosum.** Beautiful spikes of brilliant rich blue flowers, with a white centre; 2½ feet . .	5
5706 **Nudicaule.** Bright scarlet flowers; 18 inches .	10
5708 **Cashmerianum.** A beautiful dark blue . . .	10
5707 **Zalil.** A lovely shade of sulphur-yellow . . .	10
5718 **Grandiflorum Fl. Pl.** Finest double, mixed	15
5714 **Fine Mixed** single varieties. Oz. 40 cents . .	5

DIANTHUS, Hardy Pinks.

5725 **Pheasant Eye.** (*Plumarius.*) A beautiful single variety, with fringed flowers	5
5727 **Plumarius.** (*Double Scotch, or Paisley Pinks.*) Double large flowering, of various colors, mixed	10

DIGITALIS, Fox-glove.

A handsome and highly ornamental, hardy perennial plant, of stately growth, fine for shrubberies; 3 feet.

	Per pkt.
5750 **Gloxinaeflora.** Beautiful colors mixed . . .	5
5751 **Monstrosa.** Mammoth Foxglove. Mixed . .	10

HOLLYHOCKS.

For planting in rows or groups on the lawn, or for interspersing among the shrubbery, these are invaluable. We make a specialty of Hollyhocks, and the seed we offer is saved from the very best double flowers of pure and bright colors. Seed sown during the summer make strong blooming plants for the following year.

5946 **Double White.** Per oz. $1.00	10
5948 **Double Yellow**	10
5956 **Double Maroon**	10
5955 **Double Sulphur**	10
5951 **Double Bright Red**	10
5952 **Double Bright Pink**	10
5950 **Extra Choice Double, mixed,** per oz. $1.00 .	10

MYOSOTIS, Forget-me-not.

Neat and beautiful little plants with star-like flowers; succeeding best in a shady, moist situation.

6121 **Myosotis Alpestris Cœrulea.** Bright blue .	5
6122 **— Alpestris Alba.** Pure white; 6 inches . .	5
6127 **— Eliza Fonrobert.** Large flowering, bright blue; remarkably fine and distinct	5
6128 **— Alpestris Victoria.** Of bushy habit, bearing large bright azure-blue flowers; very fine	10
6125 **— Dissitiflora.** Compact habit, profuse bloomer; exquisite blue; an attractive spring bedding plant; 6 inches	10
6123 **— Palustris.** The true Forget-me-not; beautiful blue flowers; 6 inches	10
6126 **— Palustris Semperflorens.** A charming dwarf Forget-me-not, continuing in bloom from early spring until autumn; blue; 8 inches . .	10

PLATYCODON, (Wahlenbergia.)

Hardy perennials, producing very showy flowers during the whole season. They form large clumps, and are excellent for planting among shrubbery.

6360 **Platycodon, Mixed.** Blue and white	10
6361 **— Mariesi.** Large, open, bell-shaped flowers of a rich violet blue, beautiful	10
6357 **— Japonicus.** (Double Japanese Bell Flower)	15

PANSIES. Dreer's Superb Strains.

Per pkt.

This attractive plant is too well known to require any description, as it is a favorite with all. We have made careful tests of all the leading strains, and offer the following as the best in their several classes.

6238 **Dreer's Royal Exhibition.** This strain comprises a beautiful collection of colors and markings, and we are confident it will prove satisfactory for perfection of form, firmness of texture, freedom of bloom and elegance of coloring. It is the result of many years' careful selection and hybridization, and embraces all the attractive features that tend to make the Pansy the people's flower. ₁⁄₁₆ oz. $1.00 50

6219 **Giant Trimardeau.** Large flowering varieties in finest mixture . . . . , 15

6220 **Dreer's Premium.** Seed saved from first-class flowers only ; beautiful colors mixed 25

6222 **Odier** (*Five-blotched*). A beautiful strain of various colored large, perfectly formed flowers 25

6217 **French Large Stained.** Very beautifully marked varieties in finest mixture 25

6216 **Bugnot's Superb Blotched.** A beautiful class with extra large flowers, mixed colors 50

6230 **English Finest Mixed.** Per oz. $3.00 10

6240 **Good Mixed.** All colors. Per oz. $1.50 . . . 5

HARDY PERENNIAL POPPIES.

6385 **Bracteatum.** Very large orange scarlet flowers 10

6379 **Nudicaule** (*Iceland Poppy*). This is one of the most effective and beautiful. They are perfectly hardy and produce an endless profusion of flowers, useful for cutting. Mixed colors . 10

6390 **Orientale** (*The Large Oriental Poppy*). A charming summer-flowering plant, producing numerous deep crimson flowers, having a conspicuous black blotch on each petal 10

6395 **Orientale Hybrids.** Beautiful new hybrids of the Oriental Poppy, producing flowers of immense size, six inches and over in diameter and of many novel colors, salmon, pink, cherry, etc. 15

HARDY PRIMROSES.

These are among the best of the early spring blooming plants. With a slight protection they will stand the winter, but do better if protected by a cold frame.

6432 **Primula Japonica.** Bright and showy flowers; mixed colors 10

6415 **Primula Veris.** (*English Cowslips*). Flowers of different colors, very fragrant 5

6431 **Primula Vulgaris** (*Yellow English Primrose*). The common hardy English variety; flowers fragrant and of light canary color 10

CHINESE PRIMROSE.

PRIMULA SINENSIS FIMBRIATA.
FRINGED CHINESE PRIMROSE.

Per pkt.

These charming and beautiful plants are indispensable for winter and spring decoration in the greenhouse or conservatory. Our seed is, as usual, from the finest collections.

6417 **Single White Fringed** 25

6428 **Double White Fringed** 50

6418 **Single Red Fringed** 25

6421 **Punctata Elegantissima.** Crimson, spotted . 50

6422 **Kermesina Splendens.** Crimson, yellow eye 50

6425 **Alba Magnifica.** The finest pure white, with bright yellow eye, beautifully fringed 50

6424 **Holborn Blue.** A unique color 50

6440 **Fern-Leaved, Finest Mixed.** 50

6450 **Double Mixed,** all colors 50

6430 **Dreer's Choicest Mixed.** A grand strain containing only the finest varieties . . . . . . , . 25

The following varieties are of the easiest culture in green-house or light window of dwelling house, flowering abundantly and continuously.

6423 **Primula Obconica.** Profuse blooming, bearing on long stems heads containing 10 to 15 flowers ; pure white shading to lilac, and have the true Primrose fragrance 15

6484 **Primula Floribunda.** This is of the same general character as the above, differing only in color of the flower, which is a lovely shade of primrose yellow 25

POLYANTHUS, Primula Elatior.

Showy, early spring, free-flowering plants, fine for either pot or outdoor culture ; hardy perennials.

6362 **Polyanthus, English.** All colors mixed . . 10

6363 **— Duplex.** Double hose-in-hose, beautiful . 25

6364 **— Gold Laced.** Very showy and attractive . 20

SWEET WILLIAM.

A well-known free flowering plant, producing a splendid effect in beds and shrubbery with their rich and varied flowers.

6625 **Auricula Flowered.** Beautiful single varieties, all colors. Oz. 50 cents 10

6640 **Single Mixed.** Per oz. 40 cents 5

6680 **Double Mixed.** Per oz. $1.00 10

VIOLET, Viola Odorata.

Well-known fragrant early spring blooming plants for edgings, groups or borders ; thriving best in the summer in a shady situation, in a rich, deep soil.

6725 **Blue.** Sweet scented 10

6726 **White.** Very fragrant ; free flowering . . . 10

6727 **Mixed.** Blue and white 10

WALL-FLOWER.

Well-known, deliciously fragrant plants, blooming early in the spring, with large, conspicuous spikes of beautiful flowers ; should be protected in a cold frame.

6740 **Wall Flower, Single Mixed** 5

6730 **"   "   Finest Double Mixed** 10

lant Department.

Our stock of Decorative Plants is the most extensive in the country, and we are in a position to give the very best value, stock being all in prime condition. In winter-flowering plants, only varieties which have been specially grown for this purpose are offered in this catalogue, insuring good results. For a complete list and full description, please see Dreer's Garden Calendar, 1897.

ALLAMANDA WILLIAMSII.

This handsome variety is entirely distinct from all others, being quite dwarf and in no way resembling a climber, but forming a compact bush with trusses of bloom at every point. It continues flowering the whole summer, and, with proper management, in the winter also. The flowers are of a very rich yet delicate tint of yellow, and are deliciously scented. 25 cents each.

ANTHURIUM. (Flamingo Flower.)

Andreanum. A beautiful plant, with large, brilliant scarlet flowers of a leathery texture. They remain in perfection for weeks. Strong plants, $1.50 each.

Scherzerianum. One of the most striking, producing beautiful brilliant scarlet flowers, each of which remains from two to three months in bloom. $1.00 each.

Grande. Foliage bright, rich velvety green, principal veins elegantly banded with silvery white. When young, the leaves are of a violet rose color, beautifully marked. $1.50 each.

ARALIA.

Sieboldii. A most excellent house plant, having large, deeply cut foliage, which is of a bright, cheerful green color. 50 cents each.

Sieboldii variegata. A pretty variegated form of the above; 50 cents to $1.00 each.

Chaubrieri. A most graceful species with finely divided bronzy-green foliage; useful table plants. $1.50 each.

ARDISIA CRENULATA.

A very ornamental greenhouse plant, with dark evergreen foliage, producing clusters of brilliant red berries; a first-class house plant. 25 cents, 50 cents and 75 cents each.

ARAUCARIA EXCELSA. Norfolk Island Pine.

This most beautiful of all the tender evergreens is becoming more popular every season.

As a decorative plant for the house this is one of the handsomest and most serviceable plants in our collection.

4 inch pots,	6 to 8 inches high			$1.00 each.
5 " "	12 to 15 "	"		2.00 "
6 " "	15 to 18 "	"		2.50 "
7 " "	20 to 24 "	"		3.50 "

ARAUCARIA EXCELSA GLAUCA.

This is identical with the above, except in the color of the foliage, which is of a beautiful bluish or glaucous color. The plants we offer of this are exceptionally heavy fine dwarf specimens.

5 inch pots,	8 inches high		$1.50 each.
6 " "	15 "		3.50 "

ASPARAGUS.

Sprengeri. A most desirable new species, especially useful to grow as a pot plant for decorative purposes or for planting in suspended baskets; the fronds are frequently four feet long, are of a rich shade of green and most useful for cutting, retaining their freshness after being cut for weeks. It will make an excellent house plant, as it withstands dry atmosphere and will succeed in almost any position. We consider this one of the best house plants introduced for many years. 25c. ea.; $2.50 doz.

Plumosus Nanus. This graceful climbing Asparagus has to a great extent taken the place of the once popular *Smilax* in all fine decorations. It possesses the advantage of being much more graceful, its foliage being finer than that of the most delicate fern, and will last for weeks after being cut, the whole plant being of a bright, cheerful green. It is an excellent house plant, succeeding under almost any conditions. 25 cents and 50 cents each.

ASPIDISTRA.

Lurida. A very useful and durable decorative plant of strong growth; will succeed in any position; an excellent hall or corridor plant. 50c., 75c. and $1.00 each.

Lurida variegata. A pretty variegated form of the above, the foliage being striped with white. 50c. and 75c. each.

BEGONIA REX.

We have a most beautiful collection of this justly popular pot plant in twelve very handsome varieties. 15c. ea.; $1.50 doz.

BEGONIAS.

Flowering Varieties.

Haageana. We consider this the finest ornamental flowering Begonia yet introduced. It is of strong erect habit, producing naturally very symmetrical plants which are in flower the year round; the flowers, which are of the largest size, are of a creamy white with just sufficient pink to give them a bright cheerful glow, the foliage is of large size, but not coarse, is of a bronzy green above and red below; it makes an admirable pot-plant and at the same time is an excellent variety for out-door bedding.

Argentea Guttata. Foliage of large size, of rich green, spotted with silver; a beautiful variety.

Metallica. A fine erect-growing variety, with dark, rough leaves; the surface is a lustrous bronze green; veins depressed and dark red.

Rubra. Dark green leaves, flowers scarlet rose, glossy and wax-like.

Semperflorens Gigantea. Flowers brilliant carmine red, borne in large panicles well above the foliage.

Thurstonii. A distinct and pretty shrubby variety, with thick, heavy foliage, which is of a rich metallic-green above and bright red underneath; the flowers are of a fine pink, rising well above the foliage.

Price, any of the above 15c. ea.; Set of 6 varieties 75c.

ARAUCARIA EXCELSA.

BOUGAINVILLEA GLABRA SANDERIANA.

A new variety and a plant that we feel certain will become very popular as a pot plant. We give the introducer's description: "It affords us great pleasure to offer this new flowering plant. We have grown this new Bougainvillea in a greenhouse, where it has continued flowering for seven months, small and large plants alike being covered with blossoms. Even plants in thumbpots were laden with bloom. The house in which our plants have been cultivated have been a sheet of flowers from May until December. It produces as freely as a Fuchsia its dazzling *rosy crimson flowers*, lasting so long in perfection and produced in smallest pots under all conditions, in amazing profusion." 50 cents each, large plants $1.00 each.

CAMELLIA JAPONICA.

Fine bushy plants 15 inches high. A choice assortment of 12 varieties 75 cents each, $7.50 per dozen.

DOUBLE WHITE CAMELLIA.

Large plants 24 to 28 inches high, $2.00 each, $20.00 per dozen.

FANCY LEAVED CALADIUMS.

For many years the Fancy Leaved Caladiums have been a special feature of our establishment. We grow several large houses of these beautiful plants alone.

12 choice new Brazilian varieties 50 cents each, $5.00 per dozen.

12 Standard varieties 25 cents each, $2.50 per dozen.

CAREX JAPONICA VARIEGATA.

An exquisitely graceful new Japanese grass with slender green foliage edged with white. It is extremely easy to grow and makes a most excellent plant for house culture. 15 cents each; 4 for 50 cents.

NEPHROLEPIS CORDATA COMPACTA.

CROTONS.

Of this beautiful class of ornamental foliage plants we offer twelve of the finest varieties. 30 cents each; $3.00 per dozen.

CYPERUS. Umbrella Plant.

Alternifolius. 15 cents and 25 cents each.
—Variegata. 50 cents each.
—Gracilis. 15 cents each.

Cycas Revoluta Sago Palm.

These are magnificent plants of noble and majestic habit, and most impressive. They are probably the most valuable decorative plants grown, both for lawn and house decoration; their heavy glossy, deep green fronds resist alike the gas, dust and cold, to which decorative plants are frequently exposed.

Each.
Plants with stems, 4 to 6 in. high, 7 to 8 leaves, 15 to 18 in. long $1.50
Plants with stems, 6 in. high, 10 to 12 leaves, 18 to 20 in. long 3.00
Plants with stems, 8 in. high, 12 to 15 leaves, 20 to 24 in. long 5.00
Specimen plants, sizes of which will be given on application, $7.50, $10.00, $12.50 and $15.00 each.
Small plants with one and two leaves, 25 cents each.

DRACÆNAS.

Amabilis. Green, white and pale violet. 50 cents and $1.00 each.
Alba Marginata. Broad green foliage. White margin. 50 cents each.
Braziliensis. Massive rich green foliage, 30 cents and 50 cents each.
Bruanti. Dark green foliage. 50 cents and $1.00 each.
Fragrans. Magnificent bold green foliage. 50 cents and $1.00 each.
Gracilis. Narrow green foliage, edged red. 50c. ea.
Lindeni. Broad green foliage. Striped golden yellow. 50 cents and $1.00 each.
Masangeana. Similar to above but with variegation in centre of leaves instead of on edges. 50c. and $1.00 ea.
Sanderiana. Green edged white. 50 cents each.
Terminalis. Rich crimson foliage marked with pink and white. 30 cents to 50 cents each.
Youngi. Light green, changing to copper. 50 cents to $1.00 each.

FERNS.

Adiantum Cuneatum. This is the popular Maiden-Hair, fine plants at 15, 25 and 50 cents each.
A. Decorum. A companion plant to A. Cuneatum, with somewhat larger, heavier foliage. 15 and 25c. ea.
A. Farleyense. This grand variety is a queen among all Ferns, large gracefully drooping fronds, which, in the young state, assume the most varied and delicate bronzy hues, when mature, assume a deep rich green. Fine plants, 50 cents to $1.00 each; specimen plants, $1.50 to $2.00 ea.
Alsophila Australis. The most rapid growing of all the tree-ferns. 25 cents each.
Cibotium Schiedei. A scarce and beautiful tree-fern. 50 cents and $1.00 each; specimen plants, $2.50 to $5.00 each.
Cyrtomium Falcatum. Large, glossy foliage, commonly called Holly Fern. 15 and 25 cents each.
Davallia Stricta. One of the finest for growing as a decorative plant in the room or planting out. 25 and 50 cents each.
Davallia Fijiensis Plumosa. A charming evergreen Fern. 25 to 50 cents each.
Microlepia Hirta Cristata. One of the prettiest house Ferns, the foliage is of a light, pleasing green, the ends being divided into many-tasseled heads. 25 cents each.
Nephrolepis Exaltata. This is the popular Boston Sword Fern, the true long-leaved variety which is used so extensively in the Eastern States. 25 and 50 cents each.
N. Cordata Compacta. In our estimation this variety is the finest of all the sword ferns. As a fern for house culture or for window gardening, we do not known of any other variety that would give the same satisfaction. 25 cents, 50 cents and $1.00 each.
N. Davalleoides Furcans. A beautiful and distinct crested variety. 50 cents to $2.00 each.
Pteris Argyrea. One of the most useful, large, bold foliage, with broad band of white through the centre of each frond. 15 and 25 cents each.
P. Cretica Albo Lineata. A pretty, dwarf, variegated variety. 15 cents each.
P. Ouradii. A strong growing variety of compact habit, with dark green fronds. 15 to 25 cents each.
P. Tremula. A well-known, strong-growing variety; one of the very best for house culture. 15 to 25c. each.
P. Cretica Mayii. A beautiful dwarf-crested or tasseled form of *Pteris Cretica Albo-lineata.* 15 to 25c. each.
Sitalobium Cicutarium. A fine variety of easy culture. 15 to 25 cents each.

Kentia Belmoreana.

PALMS.

Palms are now indispensable in all decorations, whether for apartments, conservatories or for tropical bedding in summer. The large demand the past few years has induced us to considerably increase our facilities for propagating and growing this class of stock, and we have now thirty-five of our largest houses devoted to their cultivation alone, which enables us to supply all the leading and popular varieties at most reasonable prices. The varieties enumerated below are those best adapted for house culture.

(The heights given are from top of pot.)

Areca Lutescens. One of the most graceful and beautiful palms in cultivation; the foliage is of a bright, glossy green, with rich, golden yellow stems.

3-inch pots, 4 to 5 leaves, 12 to 15 inches high						$ .25 each.
4 " " 5 to 6 " 15 to 18 " " "						.50 "
5 " " 6 to 7 " 18 to 20 " " "						1.00 "
6 " " 6 to 8 " 24 " " "						2.00 "
8 " " 10 to 12 " 36 to 42 " " "						3.50 "

Cocos Weddelliana. The most elegant and graceful of all the smaller Palms. Its slender, erect stems is freely furnished with its gracefully arching leaves; made up of innumerable long, narrow pinnæ or segments of a rich green color. The Cocos are admirable for fern dishes, as they are of slow growth and maintain their beauty for a long time. (See cut.)

3-inch pots, 12 inches high, 50 cts. each; 4-inch pots, 15 inches high, $1.00 each.

KENTIAS.

The Kentias, both Belmoreana and Fosteriana, are the hardiest in cultivation and give better satisfaction as a house plant than any other varieties. They are of slow growth, and are not affected by the dust and dry atmosphere of the house, and were we to select one Palm only, it certainly would be a Kentia. The two varieties are of similar appearance. the former being dwarfer and more spreading, and the latter is of stronger growth with broader, heavier foliage.

KENTIA BELMOREANA. (See cut.)

3-inch pots, 4 to 5 leaves, 12 inches					$ .50 each.
4 " " 5 to 6 " 15 "					1.00 "
5 " " 6 " 20 to 22 "					1.50 "
6 " " 6 " 24 to 30 "					2.50 "
7 " " 6 to 7 " 30 to 36 "					3.50 "
7 " " 6 to 7 " 36 to 42 "					5.00 "

LIVISTONIA ROTUNDIFOLIA.

One of the prettiest Palms, especially suited for table decoration. The foliage is similar to that of *Latania Borbonica*, but smaller and gracefully recurved, forming an almost globular plant. Young plants in 3½-inch pots, 4 to 5 leaves, 8 inches high, 50 cts. each.

LATANIA BORBONICA.

Chinese Fan Palm. This popular variety is too well known to require description. We grow them in immense quantities. (See cut.)

Size of Pots.	No. Leaves.	Height.	Price Each.
3 inches.	4 to 5	12 inches.	$ .25
5 "	5 to 6	15 "	.50
6 "	6	20 "	1.00
6 "	6	20 "	1.50
7 "	6 to 7	24 "	2.50
8 "	7 to 8	30 "	5.00

Latania Borbonica.

KENTIA FOSTERIANA.

Size of Pots.	No. Leaves.	Height.	Price Each.
3 inches.	3 to 4	12 inches.	$ .30
4 "	4 to 5	15 "	.50
5 "	5	18 "	1 00
6 "	5 to 6	24 "	1.50
6 "	6	36 "	2.50
7 "	6 to 7	42 "	4.00

LATANIA BORBONICA AUREA.

A golden-leaved variety of the Chinese Fan Palm; quite rare. Thrifty young plants in 5-inch pots, with 5 to 6 leaves, about 12 inches high, $3.00 each.

Caryota Urens (*Fish-Tail Palm*). An easily grown and useful sort. 50 cts. each.

Ceroxylon Niveum. Beautiful, broad foliage, silvery white on under side; of imposing habit. $10.00 each.

Phoenix Reclinata. A strong growing form of the Date Palm, with dark green, glossy foliage; a most desirable variety.

4-inch pots, 10 to 12 inches high					$ .50 each.
5 " " 15 " "					1.00 "
6 " " 24 " "					1.50 "
7 " " 30 " "					2 00 "

— **Rupicola.** This is one of the most graceful among the smaller Palms, with wide-spreading arching pinnate leaves, broadly lance-shaped in outline, with long narrow pinnæ, the lower of which become gradually reduced to spines. 50 cts. to $2.50 each.

— **Sylvestris.** An attractive sort, deep green foliage. 50 cts. to $2.00 each.

Ptychosperma Alexandrea. One of the most rapid-growing varieties and of exceedingly easy culture. Foliage light green on the upper side with a silvery reflex; very graceful.

3-inch pots, 10 to 12 inches high					25 cts. each.
4 " " 15 to 18 "					50 "

Raphis Flabelliformis. A Japanese variety of easy culture, succeeds in almost any position. The foliage is of a very rich, dark green color; the habit of the plant is to sucker from the base, so that it forms a handsome bushy specimen. 6-inch pot, about 24 inches high, $2.50 each.

Seaforthia Elegans. One of the very best for ordinary purposes, of graceful habit, and rapid, easy growth. 50 cts. and $1.00 each.

Special Offer: We will send a thrifty young plant each of Areca, Kentia, Phœnix, Latania and Seaforthia for $1.00.

Cocos Weddelliana.

FICUS, Rubber Plant.

Elastica. The well-known India Rubber Tree, one of the very best plants for table or parlor decoration. Its thick, leathery leaves enable it to stand excessive heat and dryness.

4-inch pots, 10 inches high	$ .50
5 " " 15 "	.75
6 " " 24 "	1.25

Elastica Variegata. This is one of the finest decorative ornamental foliage plants of late introduction. In habit and growth it is like the ordinary *F. elastica*, but the leaves of this novel plant have a pleasing yellow variegation throughout. Fine plants, 4-inch pots, 10 to 12 inches high, $1.00 each.

JUSTICIA VELUTINA.

Every one knows the tall, lanky, straggling habit of the old Justicia Rosea. This new sort, which is now grown so extensively by Parisian florists, begins to bloom when the plant has only three or four leaves, and is never out of flower. If pinched back occasionally it makes a very dwarf, stocky plant, frequently covered with 20 to 50 large pink flower heads lasting a long time. The foliage is also more persistent and highly ornamental, being heavy in texture and very velvety. 30 cts. each ; $3.00 per doz.

LAPAGERIA.

Most beautiful greenhouse climbers, bearing large, pendant, waxy flowers.

Lapageria Rosea. Rich crimson. $2.50 each.
—Alba. Pure waxy white. $4.00 each.

LOTUS PELYORENSIS. Coral Gem.

This charming plant is so well thought of abroad that a prominent horticultural journal color-plated it. *The Garden* says of it : " Its slender branching habit is most striking, and the *silvery foliage* even more so. Without its flowers it might almost be described as a silvery Asparagus, but the bright, coral-red flowers, measuring two inches in length, are really beautiful, greatly reminding one of the rare and beautiful Clianthus or Glory Pea, so difficult to grow, while this gem is of the easiest possible management. Its drooping habit also makes it useful for hanging baskets. 10 cts. each ; $1.00 per doz.

OLEA FRAGRANS. Sweet Olive.

An old favorite greenhouse shrub, succeeding admirably as a house plant, producing small white flowers which are of the most exquisite fragrance. 50 cents each.

OTAHEITE ORANGE.

The best of the oranges for house culture. It is of dwarf bushy habit and bears a profusion of fragrant flowers and edible fruit.

We offer a nice lot of plants in fruit at 50 cents, $1.00, $1.50 and $2.00 each.

PANDANUS. Screw Pine.

Utilis. This is one of the most useful of our ornamental foliage plants. Excellent for the centre of vases and baskets, or grown as a single specimen.

3-inch pots, 8 inches high, each	$ .25
5 " " 15 " " "	1.00
6 " " 18 " " "	1.50

Veitchi. This is one of the most attractive of decorative plants. The leaves are light-green, beautifully marked with broad stripes of pure white, and gracefully curved.

4-inch pots, 12 inches high, each	$1.00
5 " " 15 " " "	1.25
6 " " 18 " " "	1.50

Specimen plants, $5.00 to $10.00 each.

SANSEVIERA ZEALANICA.

An elegant variegated plant, especially adapted for house decoration, thick leathery leaves standing the heat and dust of the house. 15 cents each, 4 for 50 cents.

SMILAX.

A climbing plant unsurpassed in the graceful beauty of its foliage. Its peculiar wavy formation renders it one of the most valuable plants for bouquets, wreaths, festoons and decorations. Can be easily grown in the house. 10 cents each. $1.00 per dozen. $5.00 per 100.

STEPHANOTIS FLORIBUNDA.

One of the most charming hot-house climbers, growing rapidly with long, glossy, deep-green foliage, and producing clusters of pure white deliciously fragrant flowers. 50 cents each.

STIGMAPHYLLON CILIATUM.
(Brazilian Golden or Orchid Vine).

One of the prettiest tender climbing plants in cultivation, with large yellow butterfly like flowers resembling that showy orchid *Oncidium varicosum*, the flowers are produced very freely during the entire summer months. It is especially adapted for training over the pillars or on the wall of a conservatory, but will do equally well in the open air. 75 cts. each.

ROSES FOR FORCING.

The following is a select list of the most popular forcing varieties. We wish to especially impress upon our patrons the importance of early planting. Many, if not most, failures are caused through late planting, when the roots have not sufficient time to establish themselves before the plants are expected to produce a crop of bloom.

American Beauty. An excellent rose for forcing or open air. The flowers are very double, of a deep crimson color, and very fragrant.

Bridesmaid. This beautiful rose is a sport from Catherine Mermet, possessing all the good qualities of that popular variety, but surpassing it in color, being of a darker, richer color, a deep rich pink.

Kaiserin Augusta Victoria. One of the most desirable roses. The flowers, which are produced in the greatest profusion, are of large size, of a creamy white color, shading deeper towards the centre. It is a strong, healthy grower, and popular both as a bedding variety and for forcing under glass.

La France. Splendid satin rose, the sweetest of all roses.

Mme. Caroline Testout. Strong growing Hybrid Tea. The bloom is large and double, color bright satiny pink, with rosy centre. Odorous and quite free flowering. A first-rate variety for forcing.

Perle des Jardins. Beautiful large rich yellow.

The Bride. A lovely pure white rose of the Mermet type. It is very full and double free-flowering and excellent either for forcing or for summer planting.

Sunset. Fine orange-yellow.

Souv. de Wootton. Beautiful shade of crimson.

PRICE 4-inch pots 30 cents each, $3.00 per dozen ; $18.00 per 100. 3-inch pots 15 cents each, $1.50 per dozen ; $10.00 per 100.

New Rose Souv. du Pres. Carnot. The greatest acquisition in forcing roses in years. Color, rosy white ; full double, very fragrant. 3-inch pots 30 cents each, $3.00 per doz., $20.00 per 100. 4-inch pots 40 cents each, $4.00 per doz., $30.00 per 100.

We have a fine lot of strong plants of the following Greenhouse Roses, viz.:
Marechal Neil, Lamarque, Gloire de Dijon, W. A. Richardson, 40 cents each ; $4.00 per dozen.

FERTILIZERS.

Pure Bone Flour. Ground perfectly fine, an excellent fertilizer for pot plants or beds where an immediate effect is wanted. 5 lbs. 25 cts., 100 lbs. $3.00, bbl. of 200 lbs. $5.00, ton $45.00.

Pure Bone Meal. Ground expressly for our trade. Better than Ground Bone for mixing with potting soil, as it is much finer and in better condition for giving immediate effect. 5 lbs. 25 cents, 50 lbs. $1.25, 100 lbs. $2.25, 200 lbs sack $4.00, per ton $35.00.

Bowker's Lawn and Garden Dressing. A general garden manure. May be used on all garden crops, fruits, etc. Easily applied, free from weed seeds and will give large crops. Has very little odor and is clean to handle. 5 lbs. 25c., 25 lbs. $1.00, 50 lbs. $1.75, 100 lbs. $3.00, 200 lbs $5.50.

Clay's Fertilizer. This valuable imported manure is especially recommended to all who grow either fruit, flowers or vegetables, and wish to bring them to the highest perfection. Should be used in potting soil and spread on staging of greenhouses planted with flowering plants. Bag of 25 lbs. $2.00, 50 lbs. $3.50, 100 lbs. $6.50.

Pulverized Sheep Manure. Excellent for mixing with potting soil. As a lawn top-dressing it is unequalled. 5 lbs. 25 cts., 10 lbs. 40 cts., 50 lbs. $1.50, 100 lbs. $2.50.

Bowker's Ammoniated Food for Flowers. Made especially for plants grown in the Conservatory, House or Garden. Clean, free from offensive odor. Full directions with each bag or package. Package 25 cents, by mail 40 cents, 5 lb. bag 50 cents, 50 lbs. $3.50.

INSECTICIDES.

Ant Exterminator. A most effectual preparation for the destruction of ants in lawns and pleasure grounds. Directions for use on each package. Put up in three sizes: 25 cents, 50 cents and $1.00 per package.

Tobacco Dust. A sure remedy for green fly. 1 lb. 10 cts. 5 lb. packages 25 cts.

Carbolic Acid Soap. Kills all insects that destroy animals and plants. Per cake, 10 cts.

Flowers of Sulphur. A preventive and cure for mildew. Per lb. 10 cts., 10 lbs. 60 cts.

Fir Tree Oil. Half-pint 50 cts., pint 75 cts., quart $1.50, gallon $5.00. Cannot be sent by mail.

Gishurst's Compound. For destroying green fly, mildew, thrip, mealy bug and scale. Per lb. 50 cts., by mail 65 cts.

Hellebore. Thoroughly effective. Per lb. 25c., 5 lb. $1.

Pinner's Tobacco Soap. For destroying all insects on plants and animals. Per lb. 40 cts., by mail 55 cts.

Sulpho Tobacco Soap. Rose brand. Half-pound tins 25 cts. Directions on box.

Persian or Bubach Insect Powder. For destroying roaches, ants and fleas. Per lb. 35 cts.

Pure Paris Green. Directions for use with each package. Per lb. 25 cts.

Whale Oil Soap. In 1, 2 and 5 pound cans, 20, 35 and 50 cents. Bulk 10 pounds 85 cents, 100 pounds $7.50.

Slug Shot. A safe insecticide to use and combines utility with cheapness. 5 pounds 25 cts., 10 pounds 50 cts. 100 pounds $4.25. Bbl. (235 lbs.) $8.50. Canister 15 cts.

Grape Dust. An excellent preparation for destroying mildew on grape vines, etc., either in greenhouses or the open air. 5 pounds 30 cts.

Rose Leaf Extract of Tobacco. A positive remedy for insects in greenhouses and conservatories. A very strong nicotine solution. Directions on packages. Pint 30 cts., quart 50 cents, gallon $1.50.

Nikoteen. A liquid insecticide; highly concentrated extract of tobacco, used for all kinds of insects, either by vaporizing or by syringing. One of the most economical and most powerful nicotine extracts. An ordinary sprinkling can may be used for applying, but a force pump, sprayer or syringe is preferable. One part of Nikoteen to 600 parts of water is a sufficiently strong spraying solution for all insects except scale on palms. For scale use one part Nikoteen to 400 parts water. Quart cans, $1.50.

Little's Antipest. This preparation is a sure destroyer of the Scale, Woolly Aphis and insect pests of any and all descriptions. ½ gallon $1.50, 1 gallon $2.50.

Lemon Oil Insecticide. A sweet-smelling, milk-white, soapy wash. It destroys mealy bug, scale, thrip, red spider, black and green fly, caterpillar, etc. Directions on can. ½ pint 25 cents, pint 40 cents, quart 75 cents.

London Purple. The proper proportions for using are at the rate of one pound to 150 gallons of water for spraying apple trees, excellent for the Elm Beetle. Lb. 20 cents, postpaid 35 cents, 10 lbs. $1.50, 100 lbs. $15.00.

Caterpillar Lime. (*Raupenleim.*) A sure protection to fruit and shade trees against the ravages of caterpillars, borers and insects which crawl up trunks of the trees. Properly applied it will remain unaffected by temperature or rain for three months and longer. 5 lb. cans $1.00, 10 lb. cans $1.75, 25 lb. keg, $3.75. Send for circular.

Bordeaux Mixture. (*Liquid.*) This mixture is a scientific preparation and combined in a manner heretofore unknown, as by simply adding water and stirring, it is ready for use. 1 gallon $1.00, will make 1 bbl. liquid, 1 quart 40 cents, will make 15 gallons liquid.

Powell's Improved Bordeaux Mixture. (*Dry*,) for Black Rot, Mildew and Anthracnose of Grapes, Potato Rot, Leaf Blight and Fungous diseases. 5 lbs. 40 cents, 20 lbs. $1.00. Dissolve the copper in hot water in a wooden vessel. Pour the dissolved copper into the barrel, and dilute with cold water to one-half barrel. Slack the lime; bring the same to the consistency of milk and when cool pour into the copper solution straining the same through a sieve to remove coarse particles. Stir the mixture and then fill the barrel with water. Dissolve 10 lbs. to 25 gals.

"Pillar Catter." Save your trees from the ravages of the Caterpillar and all crawling insects. Easily applied, only requiring a few tacks. Measure the circumference of the trees and buy by the yard. Endorsed by Nurserymen and Park Superintendents. Ready prepared to put on trees. Price 15 cents per yard.

Gray Mineral Ash. A non-poisonous mineral Insecticide taking the place of Paris Green and London Purple, is equally as effective, much easier prepared; and while it is thoroughly destructive to insects and vermin, it has no effect upon animals or men. Take half a pound of Gray Mineral Ash and carefully sift into one gallon of *boiling water* stirring all the time, and keep boiling for ten minutes, then pour into four gallons of cold water, leaving the undissolved residue, which is worthless, in the bottom of the first kettle. Price, 1 lb. 20 cents, 2 lbs. 35 cents, 5 lbs. 75 cents, 10 lbs. $1.25.

Leggetts Champion Dry Powder Gun.

The Champion Gun.

Paris Green, Slug Shot, and Plaster Dusters.

Knapsack Sprayers.

Leggetts Champion Dry Powder Gun is one of the best appliances for distributing dry powder. One man can cover 10 acres in one day. $7.50 each.

The Champion Gun, used on trees, with tubes attached.

An effectual and cheap duster for dry powder, 15 cts. each.

With side handle for using with pole, 10 cts. each.

For applying Bordeaux Mixture and all Liquid Insect destroyers.

Excelsior (copper,) holds 4 gallons, $12.00.

Myers' (copper,) holds 4 gallons, $10.00.

THE STANDARD PARIS GREEN DUSTER.

This new Duster will enable one man to go over several acres of potatoes in one day, perfectly distributing pure Paris Green. Very durable and of simple construction. Price, $5.00.

Powder and Spraying Bellows.

Single Cone Bellows, small $1 00
"   "   "   large 1 75
Double "   " 2 75
Spraying   "   small, $1.00, large 1 75
Sulphur   " 1 50

The Imperial Barrel Pump Spray.

Myers' Barrel Pump, the simplest arrangement for Barrel work, the working parts of the Pump are submerged. all cylinders are brass. Price, $6.50.

MYERS' BARREL SPRAY PUMP.

Complete with air chamber, agitator, suction pipe and strainer hose and Vermorel Nozzle. Pump complete $7.50.

Complete outfit as shown in illustration including air chamber. $15.00.

ASBESTOS TORCH.

Made of tin, and filled with Asbestos, can be placed on a pole to reach up into high trees.

For the extermination of tent *Caterpillars* and other vermin, will burn out the cocoons of moths, and rid trees of these pests. Soak the Torch in coal oil. Price, 50c. each.

SMALL POWDER GUN.

For hand use—only for dry powder. 10 cents.

The Myers' Bucket Spray Pump

Very powerful can be used by one person with ease, the tops of trees can be reached by the addition of extension rod of 8 feet, 50c. extra.

Price of Pump, $3.00.

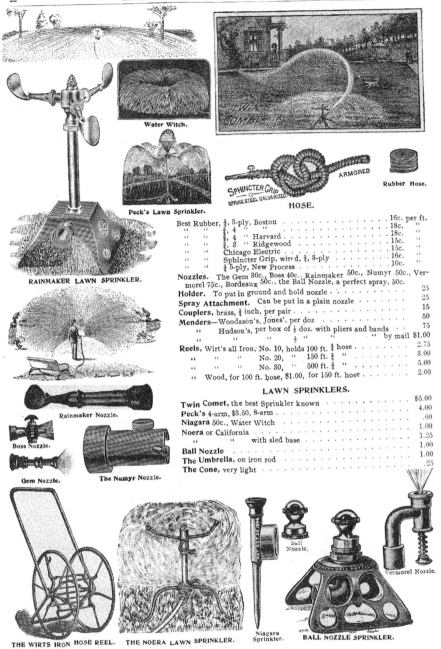

Water Witch.

Peck's Lawn Sprinkler.

SPHINCTER GRIP
SPRING STEEL GALVANIZED

ARMORED

Rubber Hose.

RAINMAKER LAWN SPRINKLER.

Rainmaker Nozzle.

Boss Nozzle.

Gem Nozzle.

The Numyr Nozzle.

HOSE.

Best Rubber, ¾, 3-ply, Boston . . . . 16c. per ft.
  " " ¾, 4 " . . . . 18c. "
  " " ¾, 4 " Harvard . . . . 18c. "
  " " ⅝, 8 " Ridgewood . . . . 15c. "
  " " Chicago Electric . . . . 15c. "
  " " Sphincter Grip, wired, ¾, 3-ply . . . . 16c. "
  " " ¾ 5-ply, New Process . . . . 10c. "

Nozzles. The Gem 30c., Boss 40c., Rainmaker 50c., Numyr 50c., Vermorel 75c., Bordeaux 50c., the Ball Nozzle, a perfect spray, 50c.

Holder. To put in ground and hold nozzle 25
Spray Attachment. Can be put in a plain nozzle 25
Couplers, brass, ¾ inch, per pair 15
Menders—Woodason's, Jones', per doz 50
  " Hudson's, per box of ½ doz. with pliers and bands . . 75
  " " " ½ " " " by mail $1.00
Reels, Wirt's all Iron, No. 10, holds 100 ft. ¾ hose 2.75
  " " " No. 20, " 150 ft. ¾ " 3.00
  " " " No. 30, " 500 ft. ¾ " 5.00
  " Wood, for 100 ft. hose, $1.00, for 150 ft. hose 2.00

LAWN SPRINKLERS.

Twin Comet, the best Sprinkler known $5.00
Peck's 4-arm, $3.50, 8-arm 4.00
Niagara 50c., Water Witch 60
Noera or California 1.00
 " " with sled base 1.25
Ball Nozzle 1.00
The Umbrella, on iron rod 1.00
The Cone, very light .25

THE WIRTS IRON HOSE REEL. THE NOERA LAWN SPRINKLER. Niagara Sprinkler. BALL NOZZLE SPRINKLER.

Ball Nozzle.

Vermorel Nozzle.

Green Tapering Stakes.

Grindstone.

White Cedar Tree Tub.

Sprinkler, Bent.   Sprinkler, Straight.

Indestructible Copper Labels.

Calf=Feeder	. . . .	$2.50
Milk Pail	. . . . . .	2.25

Grindstones. Ohio, mounted, 18 in., 50 lbs., ... 3.00
    "   "   "   20 " 75 " 3.50
    "   "   "   24 " 100 " 4.25

LABELS.

Wood, pot, painted, 3½ in., per 100, 10c.   per 1000 75
  "   "   "   4 "   "   12c.   " 85
  "   "   "   4½ "   "   15c.   " 1.00
  "   "   "   5 "   "   20c.   " 1.10
  "   "   "   6 "   "   25c.   " 1.25
  "   "   "   8 "   "   35c.   " 2.50
  "   "   " 10 "   "   50c.   " 4.00
  "   "   " 12 "   "   75c.   " 5.25
  " tree,   "   3½ " notched or pierced, per 100, 15c.,
    per 1000 . . . . 1.00
Copper, indestructible, No. 1, per doz., 20c.,   per gross . 1.50
    "   "   No. 2,   "   25c.,   "   . 2.00
Zinc,   "   No. 1,   "   15c.,   "   . 1.30
  "   "   No. 2,   "   20c.,   "   . 1.75
  " tree. Extra heavy, small, 60c. per 100 ; medium, $1.50
    per 100 ; large, per 100 . . . . 3.00
Indelible Ink, for zinc labels, per bottle 25
  "   Pencils, black, for wood labels, 10c. each ; per doz. . 1.00
Rustic Hanging Basket, oval, $1.25, $1.50 . . . . 1.75
  "   "   "   round, $1.00, ... 1.50
  "   **Chairs**, Laurel $3.50, Cedar 3.00
  "   **Settees.** Cedar, 5 ft. long, $5.00 each. Per pair . . 9.00
Sprinklers. Rubber, straight or bent neck, large 1.00

Laurel Rustic Chair.

STAKES.

				Doz.	100.			Doz.	100
Light tapering, painted green, 1½ ft.,	$0.12	$0.75	3 ft.; $	.40	$2.50
"	"	"	"	2 "	.20	1.25	3½ "	.50	3.25
"	"	"	"	2½ "	.30	1.75	4 "	.65	4.00
"	"	"	"				5 "	.75	4.75
Heavy Dahlia	"	"	3 "	.60	3.75	5 "	.90	6.25
"	"	"	4 "	.75	5.00	6 "	1.10	7.50

				100.	1000.		100.	1000.
Galvanized, Hard Steel	. . .	2 "	.70	5.50	3½ "	1.00	8.50
"	"	. . .	2½ "	.80	6.50	4 "	1.15	10.00
"	"	. . .	3 "	.90	7.50	5 "	1.40	11.50
Unpainted, for Chrysanthemums, 44 in. long, ¼ in. diam.,					.75	5.00
"	"	44 "	"	⅜ "	"	1.00	6.00
"	"	44 "	"	½ "	"	1.25	8.00
"	"	36 "	"	⅜ "	"	.60	5.00

Cane, 6 to 8 ft. long, can be cut to any desired length . . . 1.00   8.00

SYRINGES.

Brass, No. A, 1 stream and spray rose, 12 x 1 in. 1.85
  " No. C, 1 stream and spray rose, 14½ x 1½ in. 3.00
  " No. 2, 1 stream and 2 roses, 13½ x 1 1/2 in. 3.60
  " No. 3, 1   "   2   " 18 x 1½ in. 5.00
  " No. 5, 1   "   2   " 18 x 1½ in. 5.75
  " No. G. 1   "   1   " 16 x 1½ in. curved neck . . . 4.00
Brass, No. H, 18 in. long, 1½ in. diameter 2.00
  . Zinc $1.00   brass surface 1.25

Rustic Hanging Basket.

Painted Pot Labels.

Calf Feeder.   Perfect Milk Pail.

TREE TUBS.

	MACHINE MADE.				HAND MADE.		
No.	Outside Diam.	Length of Stave.		No.	Outside Diam.	Length of Stave.	
0	27 in.	24 in.	$6.75	0	27 in.	24 in.	$5.00
1	25 in.	22 in.	5.50	1	25 in.	22 in.	4.50
2	23 in.	20 in.	4.50	2	23 in.	20 in.	3.75
3	21 in.	18 in.	3.85	3	21 in.	18 in.	3.25
4	18 in.	16 in.	3.25	4	19½ in.	16 in.	2.75
5	16 in.	14 in.	2.75	5	18 in.	14 in.	2.40
6	14 in.	12 in.	2.30	6	16½ in.	13 in.	2.00
7	13 in.	11 in.	2.10	7	15 in.	12 in.	1.75
8	12 in.	10 in.	1.90	8	14 in.	10 in.	1.50

Syringes.

FRUIT PICKERS

Crider's.

Sieves.   Universal.   Wire.

Eureka Weeder.

Lang's Weeder.

Excelsior Weeder.

Hand Fork.

Grape Thinning Scissors.   Steel Trowel.   Wheelbarrow.

Oval Watering Can

Light Watering Can   Galvanized Watering Can

Livingston Tomato Trellis.

Gem Single Wheel Hoe.

Planet Jr., Double Wheel Hoe.

Iron Age Single Wheel Hoe.

Fruit Picker. Wire, 40c.; Crider's, 75c.; Universal $1 25

Forks. Hand-weeding, American, all steel 25

Trowels. Solid steel, American . 6 in., 25 cts.; 7 in. polished 50

     "   Cleves' Angle . 5 in., 10 cts.; 7 in., 15 cts.; 8 in., 20

Scissors. Grape thinning, Saynor's English, 6 in., $1.00 ;

     7 in., $1.25 ; 8 in., ... 1 50

Sieves. 18 in., 75 cents ; 20 in. 85

Watering Cans.

     Heavy American, painted green. Oval, 4 qt., $1.60 ; 6
     qt., $2.00 ; 8 qt., $2.50 ; 12 qt., $3.00 ; 16 qt., $3.50. Round,
     4 qt., $1.25 ; 6 qt., $1.60 ; 8 qt., $2.00 ; 12 qt., $2.50 ; 16 qt., 3 00

     Heavy Galvanized. Round, 4 qt., $1.50 ; 6 qt., $1.75 ; 8
     qt., $2.00 ; 10 qt., $2.25 ; 12 qt., $2.50 ; 16 qt., $3.00.
     Oval, 6 qt., $2.00 ; 8 qt., $2.25 ; 10 qt., $2.50 ; 12 qt., . . 2 75

     Light round galvanized, 4 qt., 40 cents ; 6 qt., 60 cents ;
     8 qt., 75 cents ; 10 qt., $1.00 ; 12 qt., $1.25 ; 16 qt., . . . 1 50

     Light American, painted green. Round, 1 qt., 20 cents ;
     2 qt., 25 cents ; 4 qt., 35 cents ; 6 qt., 50 cents ; 8 qt., 75
     cents ; 10 qt., 90 cents ; 12 qt., $1.15 ; 16 qt., ... 1 40

Tomato Trellis. Easily put together—durable, each 15

     cents. Per dozen 1 50

Weeders.

     Excelsior, 15 cents. Lang's, 25 cents. Eureka 25

Wheelbarrows.

     No. 2, Jacob's Patent Wheel 3 25
     " 3,   "   "   " 3 75
     " 4,   "   "   " 4 25
     " 3, Baltimore Barrows, strong, neat 3 00
     " 4,   "   "   "   " 3 50
     " 5,   "   "   "   " 4 00
     Canal Barrows, wood body 2 00
     Boys' Barrows 2 00

CULTIVATORS.

Planet Jr. Single Wheel (Hand) 4 50
     "   Double   "   " 6 00
     "   No. 8, Horse Hoe complete 7 50
     "   No. 5,   "   " 6 25
     "   Twelve Tooth Harrow (Plain) 4 90
Iron Age. Single Wheel Hoe (Hand) 4 50
     "   Double   "   " 6 00
     "   Garden Plow,   " 2 50
     "   Horse Hoe complete 5 25
     "   Diamond Tooth Harrow 4 25
Gem. Single Wheel Hoe (Hand) 3 50

TOOLS FOR THE LAWN.

The "**Hustler**" **Lawn Rake.** All steel galvanized, reversible, one of the strongest rakes made. Can be used for raking fine cut grass the reverse side for leaves, etc., 50c. ea.

The "**Automatic**" **Lawn Rake.** The only self-cleaning rake. Adapted to all sorts of work. 22 teeth, 60 cents; 26 teeth, 70 cents; 36 teeth, $1.00 ; 50 teeth, $1.50 each.

"**Lawn King**" **Rake.** A very light, out strong, wooden rake of same pattern as the "Automatic" excepting the self-cleaning attachment. 22 teeth, 40 cents; 26 teeth, 50 cents; 50 teeth, $1.00 each.

Lawn and Scarifying Rake. A rake of a special design for a special purpose, which is to cultivate the lawn. The short sharp teeth being used to comb the surface of the lawn, which is just as essential as the cultivation of garden crops. The reverse side is used for raking up cut grass, leaves, etc. 50 cents each.

"**Gem**" **Lawn Rake.** This is the old style wire lawn rake, very much improved in pattern. The teeth are heavy wire, set in wooden head. 50 cents each.

Common Wooden Lawn Rake. 14 teeth, 30 cents; 18 teeth, 40 cents; 24 teeth, 50 cents each.

Wooden Straw Rake. 12 teeth, 25 cents each.

GRASS HOOKS OR SICKLES. American. 25 cts each.

Dutch. Small, 30 cents; medium, 40 cents each.

English. Riveted back. Small, 40 cents; medium, 50 cents; large, 60 cents each.

SCYTHE, (Grass). American Clipper. 75 cents each.

American Bush or Briar. 75 cents each.

English Lawn. Riveted back, broad blade, 30, 32, 34 and 36 inches, $1.00 each.

SCYTHE STONES. Welsh Talacre. Round, 15 cts each.

Derby American. 10 cents each.

German. Fine grit, 15c. ea. **Rifles Emery.** 10c. ea.

EDGING KNIVES. American. With handle, 50 cts each. **English.** 9 inch blade with handle, $1.25 each.

GRASS BORDER OR EDGING SHEARS. For trimming the overhanging grass on edges of walks, etc.
8 inch blade, $2.00. With wheel, $2.25 per pair.
10 " " 2.25. " " 2.75 " "

Lawn Shears. For cutting grass under shrubs, fences, etc., with 2 wheels, $2.50 per pair.

Grass or Sheep Shears. Curved and straight handles. Steel, small, 35c.; medium, 50c.; large, 75c., per pair. English polished, 7½ in. blade, $1.15. With inside spring,$1.25 per pair.

DOCK LIFTERS AND SPUDS. English Daisy Grub. Blued steel, $1.25 ; wrought iron, 75c.; cast iron, 50c. each.

Heavy Dock Lifter. For field use. $1.75 each.

English Steel Spud. With walking cane handle, $1.50 ; without handle, 75 cents each.

American Steel Spud. Long handles, plain, 50 cents ; with foot rest, 75 cents each.

CLEVE'S ANGLE TROWEL. An excellent tool for cutting out weeds. 5 inch, 10 cts ; 7 inch, 15 cts ; 8 inch, 20 cts.

WRIGHT'S HANDY LAWN WEEDER. An excellent tool for extracting all kinds of weeds from a lawn. Can be used without stooping ; has a spring grip which takes hold of the weed after cutting. Directions for using with each. Price $1.

SCUFFLE HOES. For cutting weeds from walks and drives. 4 inch, 40 cts ; 5 inch, 50 cts ; 6 inch, 60 cts ; 7 inch, 65 cts ; 8 inch, 70 cts ; 9 inch, 80 cts ; 10 inch, 90 cts, each.

LAWN & SCARIFYING RAKE.

COLDWELL'S PATENT.

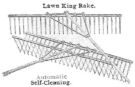

Lawn King Rake.

Automatic Self-Cleaning.

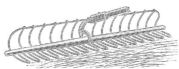

The Gem Lawn Rake.

Grass or Sheep Shear.

WRIGHT'S HAND LAWN WEEDER.

Border Shear.

English Daisy Grub.

Lawn Scythe.

Heavy Dock Lifter.

Perfection Mole Trap.

CLEVE'S ANGLE TROWEL.

Olmstead's Mole Trap.

Spud with foot rest.

Spud.

Scuffle Hoe.

Grass Edging Knife.

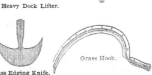

Grass Hook.

LAWN MOWERS.

Philadelphia   Continental   Imperial

HIGH-GRADE HAND LAWN MOWERS.

Continental and Pennsylvania.

LOW WHEEL.		HIGH WHEEL.	
10 inch . . . $4.50		15 inch . . . $8.50	
12 " . . . 5.00		17 " . . . 9.50	
14 " . . . 5.50		19 " . . . 10.50	
16 " . . . 6.00		21 " . . . 11.50	
18 ' . . . 6.75			

Philadelphia Mower.

10 inch $4.50
12 " 5.00
14 " 5.50
16 " 6.00
18 " 6.75

Imperial Mower.

LOW WHEEL		HIGH WHEEL	
12 inch $5.00		14 inch $7.50	
14 " 6.00		16 " 8.25	
16 " 7.00		18 " 9.00	
18 " 7.75		20 " 9.75	
20 " 8.50			

The Dreer Lawn Mower.

No Sharpening. No Setting.

Size	Net Price	Size	Net Price
10 inch cut $3.50		14 inch cut $4.50	
12 " 4.00		16 " 5.00	

Dreer Lawn Mower

Pennsylvania Horse Lawn Mower.

These famous machines have been sold throughout the country—satisfaction guaranteed. Width of cut, 30 inches. Weight, 320 lbs. It has an open cylinder, and all the bearings, including the knives, are made of solid cast-steel. The draft irons are for use either with or without the shafts, to enable the horse to walk on the cut grass.

OPEN CYLINDER

With draft irons only $60.00
" " " and seat 65.00
" " " shaft and seat 70.00

The Philadelphia Horse Mower.

30 in. cut, 315 lb. open cylinder, $60.00
30 in., 315 lb., closed cylinder 60.00
35 in., 360 lb., open cylinder 70.00
Shaft and seat to any of above, $10.00 extra.

Coldwell's Improved Horse Lawn Mower

Coldwell's Horse Lawn Mower.

This is one of the best and most perfect Horse Lawn Mowers manufactured. It is used exclusively by the Government and on the largest public and private lawns in the country. They are furnished with shafts, seat and side draft attachment (except Pony Mower), which keeps the horse on the cut grass only. Each Mower warranted to give complete satisfaction.

PRICES (STRICTLY NET).

25 in. cut (Pony Mower) $37.50 ; with shafts . . $45.00
30 in., complete with seat, shafts and side draft 60.00
35 in., complete with seat, shafts and side draft 75.00
40 in., complete with seat, shafts and side draft 90.00

All prices include packing and delivery to any Freight or Express Line in Philadelphia.

The Braun Grass Catcher.

The most perfect Grass Catcher on the market, being made with galvanized-iron bottom that will not sag and drag on ground when fitted ; can be adjusted in a moment and dumped quickly.

FOR LOW WHEEL MOWERS		FOR HIGH WHEEL MOWERS	
10 inch $1.15		15 inch $1.40	
12 " 1.25		17 " 1.50	
14 " 1.30		19 " 1.60	
16 " 1.40		21 " 1.75	
18 " 1.50			

Philadelphia Horse Lawn Mower

Horse Boots.

Prevents the hoofs from marring the lawn. They are made of strong leather, fastened with copper rivets and will wear a long time.

Flat soles, per set of four $8.00
Round soles, per set of four 9.00

HENRY A. DREER, 714 Chestnut Street, Philadelphia, Pa.

CPSIA information can be obtained
at www.ICGtesting.com
Printed in the USA
BVHW011626220219
540828BV00029B/242/P

9 780656 328758